South of the Yangtze

To Melanie Nan and Nic Gould

SOUTH of the YANGTZE

TRAVELS THROUGH THE HEART OF CHINA

Bill Porter

COUNTERPOINT

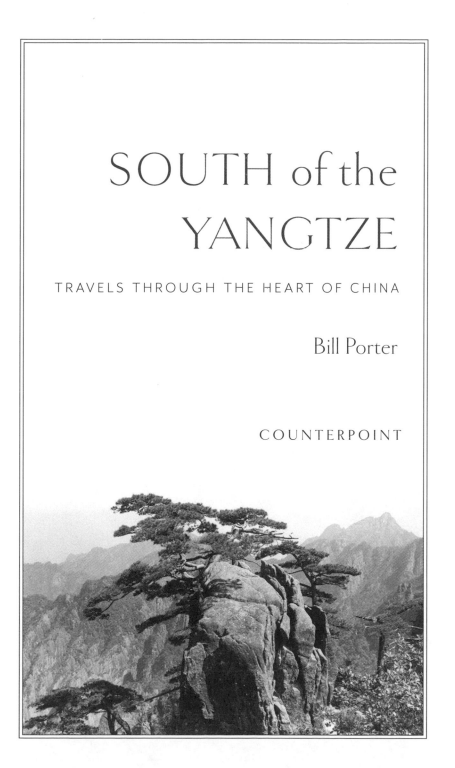

Library of Congress Cataloging-in-Publication Data
Names: Porter, Bill, 1943-
Title: South of the Yangtze : travels through the heart of China / Bill
    Porter.
Description: Berkeley, CA : Counterpoint Press, [2016]
Identifiers: LCCN 2016008978 | ISBN 9781619027343 (paperback)
Subjects: LCSH: Yangtze River Region (China)--Description and travel. |
    Porter, Bill, 1943---Travel--China--Yangtze River Region. |
    Landscapes--China--Yangtze River Region. | Yangtze River Region
    (China)--History, Local. | Yangtze River Region (China)--Social life and
    customs. | Yangtze River Region (China)--Pictorial works. |
    Black-and-white photography--China--Yangtze River Region. | BISAC: TRAVEL
    / Asia / China.
Classification: LCC DS793.Y3 P67 2016 | DDC 951.2--dc23
LC record available at http://lccn.loc.gov/2016008978

Cover and interior design by Gopa & Ted2, Inc.
Typesetting by Tabitha Lahr

COUNTERPOINT
2560 Ninth Street, Suite 318
Berkeley, CA 94710
www.counterpointpress.com

Printed in the United States of America
Distributed by Publishers Group West

10 9 8 7 6 5 4 3 2 1

Contents

South of the Yangtze

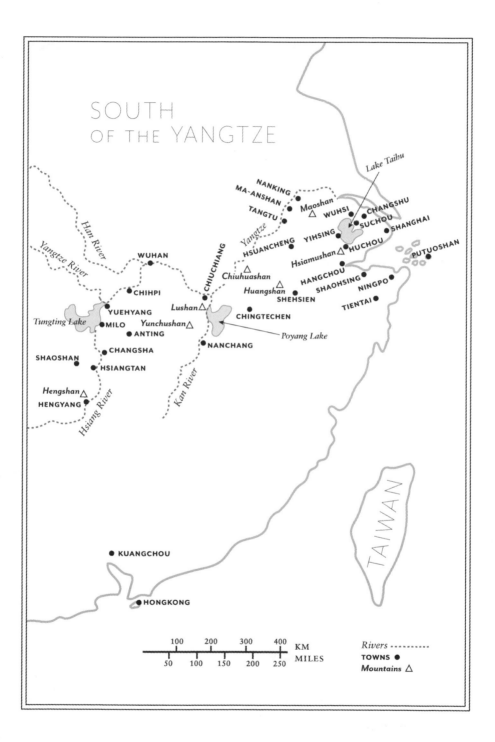

SOUTH
OF THE YANGTZE

Lake Taihu

NANKING
MA-ANSHAN
TANGTU   *Maoshan* △   WUHSI   CHANGSHU
                                        SUCHOU
                Yangtze   SHANGHAI
HSUANCHENG   YIHSING
                Hsiamushan △ HUCHOU
Han River   PUTUOSHAN
CHIUCHIANG *Chiuhuashan* △
Yangtze River   *Chiuhuashan* △ HANGCHOU
WUHAN   *Huangshan* △   SHAOHSING   NINGPO
                              SHEHSIEN
CHIHPI   *Lushan* △   CHINGTECHEN   TIENTAI
YUEHYANG
Tungting Lake MILO   *Yunchushan* △
              ANTING   *Poyang Lake*
SHAOSHAN   CHANGSHA
            HSIANGTAN   NANCHANG

Hengshan △
HENGYANG   *Hsiang River*   *Kan River*

TAIWAN

KUANGCHOU

HONGKONG

```
        100   200   300   400  KM
|----|----|----|----|----|----|
    50   100  150  200  250  MILES
```

Rivers ----------
TOWNS ●
Mountains △

廣州

1. Kuangchou

If you look at a map of China, you can't help but notice that the country is dominated by two rivers—two rivers that wander more than 5,000 kilometers, from west to east, and from the roof of the world to the sea. The river that drains North China is the Yellow River, the Huangho, while the river that drains Central China is the Long River, or Changchiang, better known in the West as the Yangtze. I suppose we

Kuanghsiao Temple and mind-flapping flagpole

Steve and Finn's plane landing at Kai Tak

could also add the West River, which drains South China. But South China has not played much of a role in the development of Chinese civilization until very recently.

Chinese civilization first developed 5,000 years ago in North China along the middle and lower reaches of the Yellow River, and that remained its center for the next 4,000 years. Then a thousand years ago, this changed. A thousand years ago, as a result of invasions from the north, the center of Chinese civilization moved south to the Yangtze. Several centuries later, the Chinese recaptured the North and once more established their capital there. But the Yangtze, not the Yellow River, has remained the center of its civilization ever since.

A thousand years ago, the Chinese came up with a name for this region. They called it Chiangnan, South of the River, the river in question, of course, being the Yangtze. The Chinese still call it Chiangnan. Nowadays it includes the northern parts of Chekiang, Kiangsi, and Hunan provinces and the southern parts of Anhui and Kiangsu. But it's not just a region on the map. It's a region in the Chinese spirit. And if you ask a dozen Chinese what "Chiangnan" means, they'll give you a dozen answers. For some, the word conjures forests of pine and bamboo. For others, hillsides of tea, terraces of rice, or lakes of lotuses and fish. Or they imagine Zen monasteries, Taoist temples, artfully-constructed gardens, or mist-shrouded peaks. Oddly enough, no one I have asked has ever mentioned the region's cities, which include some of the largest in the world. Somehow, whatever else it might mean to the Chinese, Chiangnan means a landscape and a culture defined by mist, a landscape and a culture that lacks the harder edges of the arid, ever-embattled North.

In the fall of 1991, I decided to travel through Chiangnan, following the old post roads that still connect its administrative centers and scenic wonders. I was in Hong Kong at the time, and being a foreigner, I needed a visa. This was always easy to arrange. China was next door. A visa could take as little as a day.

Once I had my visa, it was time to pack. I got out the old Forest Service backpack I had acquired in the summer of 1977 while trying to recover from hepatitis with a regimen of physical labor. I tossed in a couple changes of clothes, including a jacket for the rain—the Yangtze, after all, carries more water than any other river in the world, and that water has to come from somewhere and fall on someone. I also added a camera to record the sights I hoped to see, and a journal to record the insights I hoped to be blessed with, and a set of prayer beads for the buses, and enough money to last six weeks. I figured the trip I had in mind would cost $1500—a modest amount, as I would be sharing hotel rooms and meals with my friends Finn Wilcox and Steve Johnson.

A couple years earlier, Finn and Steve published a book together called *Here Among the Sacrificed* about the fine life of riding freight trains in America. Finn was a poet, and Steve was a photographer—not that either of them made a living doing either. Poems and photos were what they were good at. Both had to find other ways of making a living. Finn worked as a tree planter and landscape gardener. Steve worked in a boatyard repairing sailboats and fishing trawlers.

I watched their plane arrive at Kai Tak Airport. Kai Tak landings were always exciting. Whenever pilots made that final turn as they straightened out short of the runway, passengers could look just beyond the wingtips into apartment buildings and see people playing mahjong or watching TV. It was exhilarating. When Finn and Steve came through customs, they were still talking about the landing and glad to be alive. I smiled and welcomed them to Hong Kong.

Since they had already arranged their China visas in America, there was no need to linger. We headed for the train station. It was late September, but fall had yet to show up. The temperature was in the nineties. Fortunately, the express train we boarded in Hong Kong was air conditioned. It would be the last air-conditioning we would enjoy for quite a while.

The train was the express to Kuangchou. Once it left, it didn't stop until it got there. This was 1991, and the border town of Shenchen was simply that, just a border town. As we entered China, there was a big billboard with a smiling picture of Teng Hsiao-p'ing telling us that change was on the way. If it was, it hadn't reached Shenchen. At least, not yet. A few minutes later, we entered a landscape of rice fields and duck ponds and farmers dressed in black wearing broad-brimmed hats of woven bamboo. Variations of this scene continued for two hours, until the factories began to appear, and finally the high-rise apartment buildings. Two and a half hours after leaving Hong Kong, we arrived in Kuangchou. We slipped through immigration and customs so fast we felt like diplomats.

Outside the train station, we waited in line at a taxi stand. I hadn't made hotel reservations, and we considered which one to stay at. We couldn't afford the White Swan, but we wanted to stay in the same area along the Pearl River. We decided to try the Aichun, and a 10RMB taxi ride took us to its front door. It overlooked the banks of the river, and a triple with a river view cost a mere 170RMB, or 35 bucks.

The attendant unlocked the windows so that we could breathe in the air from the river. It smelled like it carried the sweat of every one of the city's three million residents. After washing off our own with a hot shower and watching the sun go down from our room, we went for a walk along the promenade. We soon found ourselves opposite one of the city's most famous restaurants: the Tatung. We walked inside and up a flight of stairs to the third floor. The place was packed. Obviously its reputation was still intact, and we did nothing to impugn it. Among the dishes we ordered was one for which it was rightfully famous: suckling pig. A modest portion cost a modest 17RMB or 3 bucks. It was so crisp and succulent we couldn't believe such food could cost so little. And it was but one dish among half a dozen.

Afterwards, we returned to the promenade and sat down on a stone bench that overlooked the river. Along the railing, two young people were leaning against each other. The only light was that of a gibbous moon. We sat there talking about the trip we were taking and the places we planned to see: the mountains, the temples, the shrines, the historical sights, even the cities, the places where people we admired had lived and died a long time ago. We agreed that paying our respects to China's poets of the past would be a highlight of our trip, assuming we could find them. In honor of this sentiment, Finn wrote his first poem:

Beneath the hanging banyans
we open three warm beers
and toast the floating moon
that lights the muddy Pearl

And so our trip began, beside the Pearl River that had been bringing travelers to Kuangchou for over 2,000 years. One traveler who sailed up the Pearl from the South China Sea was Bodhidharma. He was the man who brought Zen to China. After a three-year voyage by ship from his home in South India, he arrived in Kuangchou around 470 AD. One of the temples where he stayed was still there. It was called Kuanghsiao Temple, and it was our first destination the next morning.

After checking out of our hotel and leaving our bags at the train station, we took a taxi to the temple. Five minutes later, we walked through its huge front gate. The first thing we noticed was a well on our right. According to a sign, it was dug by Bodhidharma before he headed north, crossed the Yangtze, and eventually settled in a cave near Shao-lin Temple on Mount Sungshan. Chinese Buddhists call Bodhidharma China's First Patriarch of Zen, Zen being the understanding of what the Buddha realized by means of an intuitive, direct approach rather than a philosophical one: a cup of tea instead of a discourse.

Two hundred years after Bodhidharma arrived, a Buddhist layman named Hui-neng (638–713) also came to the same temple. Some years earlier he had traveled to a temple just north of the Yangtze to study with Hung-jen (601–674), Zen's Fifth Patriarch. Nine months later, Hung-jen decided to pass on leadership of the Zen lineage. His health was failing, and he didn't know whom to choose, so one day he called his disciples together and told them that whoever wrote a poem that best presented the teaching of Zen would become the Sixth Patriarch. The Fifth Patriarch's chief disciple wrote:

This body is a tree of wisdom
this mind is like a mirror
always keep it clean
don't let it gather dust

Stupa containing Hui-neng's hair

When Hui-neng heard this, he laughed and responded with his own poem:

Wisdom isn't a tree
the mind isn't like a mirror
there isn't anything at all
where do you get this dust

Hung-jen proclaimed him the Sixth Patriarch. This happened in 672 AD. Hui-neng, however, was an uneducated layman and not a monk. To avoid jealous rivals he returned to his home province of Kuangtung and hid out in the mountains for a number of years. Finally, one day he entered the same temple where Finn and Steve and I were standing. He noticed that people were looking at a flag flapping in the wind. Two monks were arguing about the flag: one of them said the flag was moving, the other said the wind was doing the moving. Hui-neng interrupted them and said, "You're both wrong. The only things moving around here are your minds." Everyone was stunned. The abbot then introduced himself and said, "You, sir, are no ordinary visitor. I heard the Sixth Patriarch had come south. You wouldn't be he, would you?" Hui-neng acknowledged his status and gave a sermon about the absence of duality in the realm of truth. Afterwards, the abbot offered to shave Hui-neng's head. Up to that point, Hui-neng had been a layman. Now he became a monk.

As we approached Kuanghsiao Temple's main shrine hall, we could see the flagpole where the minds of the two monks flapped in the wind 1,300 years earlier. The main shrine hall, itself, was also noteworthy. It was first built in the fourth century, and it had been rebuilt many times. We were impressed by the understated colors of its most recent incarnation. Instead of the yellow roof tiles and red pillars meant to remind people of an imperial palace, its T'ang-dynasty color scheme of gray tiles, brown pillars, and white walls imparted a feeling of simplicity and serenity. When we looked inside, we saw dozens of Chinese—and even several Westerners—meditating in front of the hall's three huge wooden buddhas.

The temple's most famous treasure, though, wasn't its shrine hall or its buddha statues. It was a small stupa outside, behind the hall. It contained Hui-neng's hair. We walked around to the back of the hall, then lit some incense and circumambulated the stupa three times. Bodhidharma and Hui-neng were our heroes, and here we were, standing in the same place where they once stood. It was a humbling, but also an exhilarating feeling, which we hoped we would be repeating in the days ahead.

After paying our respects to China's two most famous Zen masters, we walked around the temple grounds. The trees were huge, and there were signs on some. They were planted here before Hui-neng and Bodhidharma arrived and were part of a garden that belonged to an official who was banished to Kuangchou in the third century for criticizing the emperor. Among the trees he planted were bodhi trees, similar to the one under which the Buddha was enlightened. He also planted Indian almond trees, which the Chinese call k'o 柯.

During the fourth century, the official's garden became a Buddhist monastery, and it's been a monastery ever since. On our way out, we met a group of young monks who lived there. They were graduates of a famous Buddhist academy in Hsiamen and turned out to be friends of the monk who had guided Steve and me through the Chungnan Mountains south of Sian two years earlier during our search for hermits, a search that led to the writing of *Road to Heaven*. Their abbot also turned out to be a friend of Shou-yeh, the monk with whom I had first studied Buddhism in New York City over twenty years earlier. It was a small world.

I was a graduate student at Columbia University, and Master Shou-yeh had just arrived from China, via Hong Kong. He was still fairly weak from writing out the *Huayen Sutra*, the longest of all Buddhist scriptures, in his own blood. But he was there to teach, and I was there to learn. Since I was a Westerner, he kept his instruction simple. He taught me the watermelon sutra, which consisted of just one word: "watermelon." It was the only English word he knew. He told me to think about it on hot summer days. And there I was at Kuanghsiao Temple twenty years later thinking about watermelon. It wasn't summer. But

Calligraphy of Su Tung-p'o: Six Banyans

it was hot. As we walked back out the temple's front gate, waiting for us across the street was a fruit stand and slices of watermelon—courtesy, no doubt, of my old master.

After quenching our thirst, we walked several more blocks to another place associated with Hui-neng. It was called Liujung Temple, Temple of the Six Banyans. The first thing we noticed, though, wasn't its banyans but its nine-story pagoda. It was erected in 537, about fifty years after the temple was built. Locally, it was known as the Ornate Pagoda, to distinguish it from the minaret of the mosque several blocks to the south. The mosque was built in 627 by an uncle of Mohammed, which made it the oldest mosque in China. But its minaret was an unadorned, smooth-faced structure, and only twenty-five meters high, in contrast with the temple's multi-tiered sixty-meter tower.

Over the entrance were the words SIX BANYANS. The calligraphy was that of Su Tung-p'o, one of China's great poets and calligraphers. Su visited the temple during his exile in the year 1100, a year before his death. When Su visited, there were six trees in the courtyard to the left of the pagoda. Hence, he wrote the characters *Liu Jung*, or Six Banyans, to commemorate his visit. Two of the trees were still here, shading the courtyard that stretched between a pavilion and a shrine hall honoring Hui-neng, the Sixth Patriarch. Inside the hall was a bronze statue cast in 989 from Hui-neng's mummified body. He looked so thin we couldn't help thinking about lunch.

We were in luck. Three blocks away was Kuangchou's most famous vegetarian restaurant. It was called Tsaikenhsiang, and it served dishes that looked like meat and tasted like meat but weren't meat. They were made of tofu and wheat gluten and mushrooms, and everything we ordered tasted great. But we needed something to wash it down, and ordered beers. We were disappointed to learn that they didn't serve alcohol. It was a Buddhist restaurant and beer wasn't allowed. We sighed and paid the bill and considered our options.

If it had been closer to sunset, we could have taken a taxi to Jenmin Bridge and boarded a Pearl River cruise. But it was early afternoon, and we thought a park might be nice. There were three downtown and all of them within the shortest of taxi rides. The closest was Orchid Park. As its name suggested, it was devoted to orchids. And the price of admission included a pot of tea. It wasn't beer, but suddenly tea sounded good. Another possibility was the huge, rambling sprawl of Yuehhsiu Park just east of Orchid Park. It had something for everyone: man-made lakes, endless paths, the city museum, and statues of the five goats that brought the five immortals who founded Kuangchou more than 2,000 years earlier. There was also the less frequented oasis of Liuhua Park and its palm-lined pathways.

Normally, any of the three would have been fine. All we wanted to do was relax. But the weather was so stifling we decided to escape the city altogether. Instead of going to one of its parks, we hired a taxi to take us to Paiyunshan, whose forested slopes overlooked the city from the north. Surely, we thought, there was cool air waiting for us up there somewhere. Twenty minutes later, we were there, or at least we were at the foot of the mountain. The name alone, White Cloud Mountain, made us feel as if we had entered another world.

Six Banyan Temple Pagoda

Teatime at Nine Dragon Spring

In former days, the mountain was covered with Buddhist and Taoist temples and shrines. Nowadays, the only buildings on Paiyunshan were villas, teahouses, and pavilions. Halfway up, we asked our driver to stop at the former site of Nengjen Temple. As recently as a hundred years ago, the temple housed 500 monks whose practice included martial arts. The temple was destroyed during the Second World War, but the stones that made up its former foundation were still visible through the vines and the weeds. We walked past the ruins and up a flight of steps to a newly-constructed teahouse. Its white walls were lined with tastefully wrought teapots and bonsais, and there were chairs and a dozen wooden tables set beside the windows where visitors could enjoy the view of the lily-filled ponds and the lush foliage that surrounded the place.

The teahouse was named after Tiger Run Spring, which has been famous among tea cognoscenti for its water since the Sung dynasty a thousand years ago. We stayed long enough to sample the water, but the spring was only halfway up the mountain, and we wanted cooler air. We returned to our taxi and continued. Shortly before the summit, we turned off on a side road that ended at Chiulungchuan, or Nine Dragon Spring. Finally, we found what we were looking for: cool air and spring water.

Nine Dragon Spring is one of the most famous springs in South China. People have been coming here for over a thousand years. It's surrounded on three sides by the forested summit of Paiyunshan. And beyond the pines and bamboo are the distant, high-rises of Kuangchou, faintly visible through the smog. We sat down at one of the mahogany tables on the stone balcony and ordered a pot of Tiehkuanyin, or Iron Goddess tea. The setting was so relaxing, we just sat there drinking the beverage some say arose from Bodhidharma's eyelids, catching up on our journals. Two hours later, when the tea became too weak for another infusion, we headed back down. As we approached the foot of the mountain, we drove past Deer Lake and noticed two old men fishing. At least their poles were fishing. The fishermen were asleep. We smiled, glad in the knowledge that at least someone in Kuangchou knew how to spend a hot autumn day. We would have joined them, but we had a train to catch.

衡陽 衡山

2. Hengyang & Hengshan

Train tickets out of Kuangchou weren't easy to come by, especially soft sleeper berths. Fortunately, before Finn and Steve arrived, I managed to find a travel agent in Hong Kong who was able to procure three of these rarest of commodities. After reclaiming our bags at the train station luggage depository, we boarded the evening express and enjoyed a night of listening to our motel on wheels *clickety-clack* its way

Huai-jang's grave

across the Nanling Mountains that divided the area known as Lingnan, or South of the Ridges, from Chiangnan, or South of the Yangtze. Lingnan included the provinces of Kuangtung and Kuangsi and the southern parts of Hunan and Kiangsi. But Lingnan would have to wait for another trip. This time, we were bound for Chiangnan.

Sometime during the night, we crossed the mountains and just before dawn arrived at our first stop: Hengyang. As we walked outside the station, we were met by several early-bird travel guides who wanted 100RMB, or $20, for a half-day tour of their fair city. Apparently, Hengyang wasn't worth a full day.

We ignored them and boarded a local bus destined for the city's long-distance bus station, where we planned to deposit our bags. A few stops later, as we pulled away from the curb, one of the passengers asked me if I was missing something. When I said, "No," he suggested I check my pocket. Sure enough, my wallet was gone. When I asked him where it was, he pointed outside the window. A young man was walking away from the bus stop and counting my money. I yelled for the driver to stop, but he just shrugged and hit the gas. I said good-bye to my wallet. Fortunately, there was only about 50RMB, or ten bucks, in it. I kept my big money in my backpack. I felt sorry for the pickpocket and a little embarrassed that I had lowered the high regard in which he obviously held foreigners.

A few minutes later, we got off at the city's long-distance bus station and stashed our gear. I haven't mentioned it before, but when traveling in China, you'll need to deposit your bags somewhere while sightseeing. Every train station and bus station has a storage area—just make sure you ask what time it closes so that you don't have to spend a night away from whatever it is you might need in your bag. You can also try hotels or restaurants or even a store with a secure area—behind the counter usually works just fine. It's no fun lugging your bag around all day long.

Our next problem was to find transportation for the day. The easiest way to visit a number of places in a limited amount of time is to hire a taxi. Usually this involves negotiation, which I've never been very good at. But in Hengyang we were rescued from this tiresome

Hengshan's old pilgrim trail

process. While we were walking away from the bus station, I stopped to ask a policeman directing traffic. He not only flagged down a taxi, he helped negotiate the reasonable rate of 60RMB for a half-day tour. The memory of my lost wallet vanished. Hengyang was back on my good-place-to-visit list. And so off we went to see the sights, which began with Shihku Park.

The park was located at the northeast corner of the city at the confluence of the Hsiang and Cheng rivers. The Hsiang is the biggest river in Hunan—which we entered during the night, and people still refer to the province by the river's name. It's also the character used on Hunan license plates. But the reason we wanted to visit the park wasn't the river, it was Confucius. A thousand years ago, this was the location of one of the most famous academies established to study his teachings. It was called Shihku Academy, and we were hoping there was something left.

As we got out of the taxi, we were glad to see that the park was open. We thought we might be too early. We looked at a map just inside the park entrance then headed for the academy. It was built on a rocky promontory that became an island in the summer when the two rivers reached their highest levels. Hence, access was via a bridge. Alas, when we reached the bridge, the gate was closed. It was just after seven, and the academy didn't open until eight. All we could see were the white walls and black-tiled roofs of its Sung-dynasty architecture. The buildings and their setting were quite lovely, like a painting. But we had to content ourselves with the view from the bridge and soon tired of that. Normally, we would have waited, but we had big plans that day, and the sights of Hengyang were just the beginning.

On our way back to our taxi, we walked past dozens of people doing their morning exercises. Most were doing various forms of Taichichuan, but not everyone. There was one group of about thirty people learning to dance to the strains of "The Tennessee Waltz." We thought about joining them, but once again, we had to remind ourselves about the big day we had planned.

From Shihku Park, we drove to Yuehping Park. It was laid out around a man-made lake instead of a pair of rivers, but that wasn't why we were there. The park was the location of the city's museum, and I've always found such places to be sources of information that often doesn't reach the world beyond. This time we arrived just after eight, and it was open. As a museum, it was a failure. The only relief was an exhibition of blurred photographs of the wild two-footed hairy creature seen from time to time in China's more mountainous regions—the one Westerners call Bigfoot or the Abominable Snowman.

I've always thought it ironic that most of the sightings of this creature in China have been in the Shennungchia Mountains of neighboring Hupei province. A number of Taoist masters have told me that there are 600-year-old Taoists living in the same range. I've since concluded that China's two-footed hairy creature was nothing more than your basic Taoist immortal in need of a haircut. Several years earlier a Taoist doctor on Wutangshan offered to lead me into those very mountains to meet his own master, who was 250 years old, he said. Unfortunately, I was on a different mission then and didn't have time to take advantage of such an opportunity. Once again, I had other plans.

Having seen what there was to see in the museum, we returned to our taxi and told the driver to take us to one more park. In addition to serving as a gateway to South China, Hengyang was near the entrance to one of China's most famous mountains: Hengshan. In fact, the city's name, Hengyang, refers to its position on the southern, *yang*, side of the mountain. Usually when people talk about Hengshan, they refer to the half-dozen peaks that make up its center. But Hengshan is much bigger. Its peaks are said to begin as far north as the provincial capital of Changsha and extend south for 150 kilometers as far as Returning Goose Peak, or Huiyenfeng, which rose before us at the end of Hengyang's Chungshan Road.

Returning Goose wasn't much of a peak, maybe thirty meters higher than the town, but it was still counted as the southernmost of the range's seventy-two summits. The peak was now part of a park, and it had been enhanced by chicken wire and cement, and a man-made waterfall that flowed from dawn to dusk. We were there on a Sunday, and it looked like everyone in town was on the peak. At one end of the park, there was a temple full of worshippers burning paper money and lighting candles and firecrackers. And at the other end there was a sideshow with loudspeakers blaring music that might best be described as Jimi Hendrix played backwards. After a few minutes, we decided it was time to head for the real peak. We returned to the bus station, paid the driver, grabbed our gear, and boarded the next bus headed north.

As the bus began winding through a landscape of green hills, yellow rice fields, and red earth, we got our first glimpse of the countryside that characterizes the Chiangnan region. A cool breeze blew through the bus windows, and the road was smooth, which wasn't surprising—the smooth part. We were on the Kuangchou–Beijing Highway, the first cross-country highway built in China. About ten minutes north of Hengyang, we saw a mountain in the distance. It was big. A few minutes later, Hengshan's central peaks came into view. For the next fifty minutes, we continued north along the mountain's eastern flank. As we did, the mountain kept getting bigger. After winding our way through one last valley, the bus dropped us off three kilometers from the foot of the mountain.

From where we got off, there was a road on our left that led to the mountain, and we began following it. But once more we needed to deal with our gear. There was no way we were going to haul it up the mountain. Fortunately, a hundred meters down the road, there was another road that forked to the right and that led past a gauntlet of tourist shops and small hotels, one of which agreed to look after our bags.

With our gear taken care of, we headed for the mountain. But first some background. Hengshan has another name: Nanyueh, the Southern Sacred Mountain. Over two thousand years ago, Chinese Taoists came up with the theory that everything can be divided into Five Elements or Aspects. There are five musical tones, five colors, five elements, even five directions—which include the four cardinal points and the center.

Buddhists have their sacred mountains too. But Buddhism doesn't share Taoism's shamanistic roots. It was shamanism that provided the basis upon which the worship of mountains developed in China. When the country's early emperors started conducting sacrifices at mountains, five were chosen for special veneration. And 1,500 years ago, Hengshan joined this exclusive club, displacing another peak much farther north.

In the past, when emperors or their emissaries came to worship the country's sacred peaks, they did so with great ceremony in huge temples built expressly for the purpose. And so, a temple was built near the foot of Hengshan soon after it joined the big five. The temple had been destroyed and rebuilt many times since then, but it was still there at the edge of the village that had grown up around it to serve pilgrims. As we walked down the village's only paved street, we stopped to buy a few snacks for the trail, like peanuts and cookies. Then we joined the other pilgrims and entered the temple's front gate and passed through a succession of archways and shrine halls.

The buildings were relatively new and dated from 1882, which might be old in America but is yesterday in China. Still, they looked old. Finally, we reached the great hall of the Southern Mountain. The hall was among the most impressive in China, with seventy-two huge stone pillars holding up an equally huge tiled roof. The number 72 corresponded with the number of peaks that made up the 150-kilometer-long mountain. Inside was a statue of Chu-jung Huo-shen, the mythical emperor who bestowed fire on humankind. Again, this was in accordance with the theory of Five Elements, which associated the southern quadrant with the element of fire.

Speaking of fire, there was a huge blaze rising from the incense burner in front of the building, as pilgrims lit bundles of incense, not individual sticks, but bundles containing hundreds of sticks. We lit a few sticks ourselves and paid our respects to Chu-jung, then continued on. After visiting the main hall, we proceeded to a smaller hall behind it. While I was taking a photograph, I glanced down to find an old lady's hand inside my pocket about to remove its contents. I never carry much money in my pockets, but after traveling in Hunan, I carry less. Twice in one day was too much. Still, there wasn't much I could do. As soon as my eyes met the old lady's, she turned and hurried away empty-handed.

Shrine to Chu-jung Huo-shen

She must have been seventy, but I was surprised how quickly she disappeared into the crowd. Once again, all I could do was laugh.

Having paid our respects to the mountain, we thought it was time to hit the trail, or should I say road? We considered our options. Were we going to walk, or were we going to take the bus? Hengshan was unique among China's five sacred mountains in having a paved road that ended just short of the summit. Buses left every fifteen minutes, or as soon as they were full. For those who prefer to walk, it's worth keeping in mind that the trail parallels the road. In fact, for most of the way, the trail is the road, or vice versa. Hence, would-be hikers have no choice but to endure bus fumes and air horns. And for what? We didn't see much sense in walking up the mountain under such conditions.

There was an alternative, though. We learned about it from the man who operated the hotel where we stashed our bags. We followed his suggestion and started up the road that began behind the shrine halls. After about a kilometer, we stopped short of a reservoir. Past the reservoir was a martyrs' shrine built by the Nationalist Army to commemorate those who died resisting the Japanese. Instead of walking past the reservoir and the martyrs' shrine, we turned off the main road onto a dirt road on the left that led about 200 meters to a small hydroelectric station. The station looked more like a farmhouse, but it actually generated electricity from an adjacent stream. We crossed a plank bridge to the other side of the stream and followed a dirt trail into a pine forest. The trail soon disappeared, and we had to zigzag our way up a series of gullies. The man who told us about this shortcut told us not to worry about which gully we walked up. They all reconnected with the old trail—the one pilgrims took before there was a road. And he was right. After about an hour, we found ourselves back on a trail. Soon after that, the trail crossed a ridge and brought us to the front steps of Nantai Temple.

We paused at the steps to catch our breath then walked through the front gate. The temple was being renovated, and there were piles of logs and stones everywhere. Nantai was one of the most important temples in the history of Zen, and it was being restored. The temple dated back to the beginning of the sixth century, but it didn't become famous until two hundred years later when a monk named Hsi-ch'ien arrived. He was a disciple of Zen's Sixth Patriarch, Hui-neng, whom we met the day before in Kuangchou. Hsi-ch'ien came to Hengshan to study with another disciple of Hui-neng, a monk named Huai-jang. Huai-jang lived at another temple farther up the mountain, but Hsi-ch'ien preferred Nantai, and while he was here he picked up the name Shih-t'ou.

Before entering the temple's main shrine hall to pay our respects to Shih-t'ou, we stopped at the monastery store just inside the entrance and bought several cloth shoulder bags, the kind used by monks and nuns when they travel between temples or go on a pilgrimage. They were embroidered with the name of the temple, and we thought our Zen friends in America would appreciate such souvenirs. I thought mine might help protect me from pickpockets in the future. The bags had zippers inside.

As we left the monastery store, we had to step carefully to avoid the logs, bricks, and stones that filled the temple's courtyard. The buildings were being renovated. When we finally reached the entrance of the main shrine hall, there was an old lady sitting outside on a stool who insisted on reading our palms. She had never read a foreigner's palm, and she wanted to see if there was any difference. Apparently, there wasn't. After all, we're all going to die, sooner or later. In our case, she said we were going to live to be between eighty-five and ninety-five. We couldn't imagine living that long. We were hoping to die a bit earlier than that, before our bodies deteriorated to the point where someone else had to wipe our butts. But maybe she was wrong.

We thanked her anyway and entered the hall. Inside, we met an old monk talking to several laywomen. The monk turned out to be the abbot, Pao T'an. He said he was sixty-six and he had lived there as a monk since he was nine. While we were talking, someone rang a bell. He said it was time for lunch, and he invited us to join him. It wasn't as fancy as the vegetarian food we had in Kuangchou, but it was good. Afterwards he invited us to join him in his quarters for tea. While we were exchanging Buddhist gossip, he told us this story, which began when we asked him if Shih-t'ou's remains were at the temple.

Pao T'an said, "No, not anymore. Shih-t'ou wasn't cremated. His body was put in a large earthenware pot then placed inside a stupa on Purple Cloud Peak about two kilometers from the temple. One night three years ago, some thieves knocked down the stupa searching for treasure. They could have saved their effort. It had already been cleaned out by the Japanese in 1943. I was just a young monk then. The Japanese, you know, also venerate Shih-t'ou as the founder of their Soto Zen lineage. It's still the biggest Zen sect in Japan. Well, the Japanese sent Shih-t'ou's body, earthenware pot and all, back to Japan. We've tried to get it back. But it's no use, the Japanese won't give it up. But what's strange is that they've conducted experiments on Shih-t'ou's preserved remains. They've inserted needles and removed what they say is fresh tissue from his 1,200-year-old body." I was glad he told us this story after lunch and not before.

But Pao T'an wasn't done with Shih-t'ou. After we finished our tea, he led us outside the temple's front gate and pointed to a huge sloping rock face. He said that was where Master Shih-t'ou meditated and that was why he was called Shih-t'ou, which meant "rock." I should note that when I visited this same temple eight years later the entire rock face had been paved over to make a parking lot. So it goes.

We thanked the abbot for his kindness and for taking the time to talk with us. After saying good-bye, we continued up the trail. As we did, the dirt trail that brought us there became a dirt road. This was the road that brought all the building materials to the temple. It also led to the main road that brought pilgrims and tourists up the mountain as well. We followed it for a few minutes then stopped. There was a side trail on the right. Before we'd said good-bye to Pao T'an, he told us the trail led to the grave of Hui-ssu, and so we followed it.

Hui-ssu came to Hengshan two hundred years before Shih-t'ou. After paying our respects at his pine-encircled grave, we returned to the dirt road and continued on to his temple. It was to the left, just off the dirt road, and is called Fuyen. Along with Nantai, it's one of the most famous Buddhist temples in China. When Hui-ssu came here in 567 AD, he brought with him more than forty disciples. Among them was

Grave of Hui-ssu

a monk named Chih-yi. After Hui-ssu died, Chih-yi left Hengshan and moved to Mount Tientai, where he founded his own school of Buddhism. Along with Zen and Pure Land, Tientai Buddhism—as it has since been called—has remained one of the religion's major schools, in China as well as in Japan. It began, though, not on Tientai, but here on Hengshan at Fuyen Temple.

In the past, people reached Nantai and Fuyen by following the old trail that came up the mountain from the south. We were told that no one took the old trail anymore. It was too overgrown. As we approached Fuyen's front gate, we stopped to talk with a nun who was hammering the rinds off gingko nuts from trees Hui-ssu planted here fourteen hundred years ago. She stopped hammering long enough to show us a trail that led behind the temple to a cliff. The cliff was only fifty meters from the temple, but it took a few minutes to work our way through the undergrowth. Finally, we saw what she thought we wanted to see. Carved into the rock face was the calligraphy of the T'ang dynasty chancellor Li Mi. The three huge characters he wrote during his visit to the temple in the eighth century said, "Highest Light 極高明." He was refer-ring to the brand of Zen taught at Fuyen by Huai-jang.

Huai-jang was a disciple of Hui-neng, Zen's Sixth Patriarch. Follow-ing Hui-neng's death in 713, Huai-jang moved to Hengshan and finished what Hui-neng started. His disciples included the founders of most of the major Zen schools that developed in China, including Shih-t'ou, whom we met earlier on our way up the mountain at Nantai. Another disciple was Tao-yi, or Ma-tsu, as he is better known. Ma-tsu also came to Huai-jang for instruction.

One day Huai-jang saw Ma-tsu sitting just up the trail from the tem-ple meditating. Huai-jang walked over and asked Ma-tsu what he was doing. When Ma-tsu said he was meditating, Huai-jang asked him what he expected to accomplish. Ma-tsu said he was trying to become a buddha. Huai-jang bent down and picked up a brick, and started grinding it on a rock. Ma-tsu asked Huai-jang what he was doing. Huai-jang said he was trying to make a mirror. Ma-tsu laughed and said he was crazy. Huai-jang laughed back and said, so are you, trying to become a buddha by medi-tating—his point being that there's more to buddhahood than meditation.

When we walked back to the temple, the same nun was still cracking gingko nuts. Since the day was getting late, we asked her if we could spend the night at the temple. She said Fuyen was now a nunnery, and men were not allowed to stay overnight. She said to keep walking. There was a hotel up the road. We thanked her for the directions and continued on.

A few hundred meters farther on, there was a large flat boulder at the side of the road with the words Mirror Grinding Rock 磨鏡台. I was always amazed to find places where something happened a thousand years ago that someone had commemorated with a marker. But that was the way things were in China. People remembered the past. And the past was five thousand years long. After taking a picture of the rock, we continued on for another hundred meters and stopped again. Off to the side was Huai-jang's grave. We walked over and lit some incense. While we stood there waiting for it to burn down, I saw a brick in the bushes. I picked it up and put it in front of the grave. I figured Huai-jang would know what to do with it.

Calligraphy of Li Mi

Mirror Grinding Rock

When the incense finally burned down, we returned to the road. This time we didn't go far. The sun was setting, and in the middle of the forest there was a hotel. The sign on the outside said MIRROR GRINDING ROCK HOTEL. We couldn't believe our good fortune. We walked inside and asked if we could spend the night. According to the man at the front desk, we had our choice of rooms. The place was nearly empty, and rooms were only 50RMB, or $10. When we asked if there were any other hotels in the area, he said the next one was another hour up the road. Indeed, the gods had smiled upon us. After checking in, we walked up to our room. The beds were comfortable enough, and the windows looked out through pine trees at mist floating up from below. It was a lovely setting. But when we tried to take baths, we were not so fortunate. There were only three other guests at the hotel that night, not enough to warrant heating the water. We had to make do with cold showers, but at least we were able to wash off the day's dust and sweat.

Dinner was also disappointing. With so few guests, the kitchen staff was down to one person that night, and he was not a good cook. Still, at the end of a long day, food is food. We filled up on fried rice. Afterwards, on our way back to our room we decided to walk up to the next floor to see if there was a better view. The view was about the same. But the floor attendant led us to another set of stairs that led up to the roof. He was even kind enough to bring us a small table and three chairs and a dozen bottles of beer. Sitting there enjoying the view of the clear sky and the fog-shrouded mountain below made up for the cold shower and the dismal dinner. The beer, however, did not. We liked to think we had never met a beer we couldn't drink, but Hunan beer would have been an exception. Had it not been for the date, we wouldn't have drunk any of it. But it was the end of September, and that night just happened to be the Moon Festival. As we watched the biggest, brightest, most beautiful moon of the year cross the sky, we drank every one of those twelve otherwise forgettable beers.

Naturally, the next morning we got up late, with Hunan beer hangovers. It was almost noon when we checked out. At least the road beyond

Ma-ku with deer and peach, symbols of immortality
(photo by Steven R. Johnson)

the hotel was paved, and it was fairly level. We walked for about twenty minutes and saw a trail on the left that led to several of the mountain's peaks. But we kept going. A few minutes later, we came to a small reservoir. Jutting up from the stream that fed the reservoir were half a dozen huge cement mushrooms. We were so surprised, we didn't know what to think. What were cement mushrooms doing on the mountain? We didn't have an answer and continued on. A few minutes later, we came to a side trail on the left and a sign announcing that this was the Wonderland of Ma-ku.

Finally, we had an answer to our quandary about the mushrooms. Magic mushrooms have long been a favorite food of Taoist immortals. And Ma-ku was one of China's most famous. She lived here two thousand years ago, and she was known for her mushroom wine. We followed the side trail to a waterfall where her statue poured her magic wine from a jug into the stream. We cupped our hands and drank the water, hoping to float the rest of the way up the mountain. But all we felt were our hangovers from the previous night's beer.

We returned to the road, but we didn't continue in the direction we had been walking. Less than a kilometer away, the road we were on rejoined the main road. We could hear buses honking in the distance. We decided to return to the trail we had passed earlier just before the reservoir. It was an old trail and consisted of stone steps. We followed it through a pine forest and along the lower slopes of Discarded Bowl and Sky Pillar peaks. There were side trails leading to both, but we weren't about to climb any peaks. Besides, they were all shrouded in mist. We stayed on the main trail that skirted the two peaks. Finally, after several hours of plodding along and doubting our choice of trails, we reached Sutra Repository Temple. It was completely covered by fog, and whatever light there was in the sky was nearly gone. We were hoping to find a hostel of some kind to spend the night. Instead, we found a temple.

Sutra Repository Temple was first built by our old friend Hui-ssu in 568, the year after he built Fuyen Temple farther down the mountain. This was where Hui-ssu's disciple Chih-yi collated his master's works after his

Ma-ku's cement mushrooms

death before going off to Tientai to found his own school of Buddhism. Chih-yi's fame rested on his arrangement of all the sutras in the Buddhist canon in a way that showed the progression of the Buddha's teaching, and this was where he made his initial version of that arrangement.

The temple had fallen on hard times and was down to one solitary, very lonely shrine hall. We arrived just in time to join the temple's three monks for evening services, which they conducted in candlelight. Afterwards, we asked if we could spend the night. They said they didn't have any spare rooms, but there was a small hostel less than a hundred meters away. Once more, we were in luck. The hostel turned out to be a two-story stone building set around a small inner courtyard. The caretaker showed us to a room on the second floor and gave us candles. There was no electricity. Afterwards, he led us to a small hut across from the temple. The hut had a stove, and the caretaker cooked us a memorable meal, candlelit and featuring bowls of rice along with a plate of stir-fried cabbage and mushrooms and another of scrambled eggs and tomatoes. And we washed it all down with the caretaker's last four dust-covered beers. They were also from Hunan, but they tasted a lot better than the beers we had the previous night. Maybe we were just thirsty. Or maybe they had improved with age.

Afterwards, we collapsed on our cots. The moon was just as big as it had been the previous night. But we were too tired to care. The next morning, before we left, the caretaker told us we had spent the night in the same guesthouse used by Sun Yat-sen and later by Chiang Kai-shek during their visits to the mountain. He said this was where important dignitaries stayed in the old days. He pointed out the iron tiles that covered the roof. They were stamped with the date 1937. He said the tiles were made of iron because it got windy on the mountain.

The reason we were there was that we had been sneaking up the mountain along its western ridge, visiting the only functioning Buddhist temples not destroyed during the Cultural Revolution and avoiding the crowds and buses that plied the main road to the summit. But we had gone as far as we could. It was time for us to rejoin the masses. After a breakfast of rice porridge and pickles and fried eggs, we set out for the main road. Two hours later, our trail and the road met at a place called Nantienmen, or South Sky Gate.

I had seen this same name on other mountains. The reason behind it was that the ancient Chinese associated long life with the south and with a particular star in the south, namely Canopus in the constellation Carina. Anyone seeing this star was guaranteed of living to a ripe old age. Unfortunately, Canopus is a southern circumpolar star, and even though it's the second brightest star in the heavens after Sirius, it's only visible in the central part of China around the Lunar New Year and then just barely. To increase one's chances of seeing it, many people climb mountains during the Lunar New Year, and star viewing terraces were common in ancient China: hence the ubiquitous gates to the southern sky.

We stopped to catch our breath, but we didn't linger. This was also where buses turned around, and the place was piled with garbage. In fact, it stunk. We continued on toward the summit, us and a few hundred other people. Half an hour later, just before we reached the pile of garbage that covered the top, we stopped to check out accommodations at Shangfeng Temple and at several small hostels operated by different government agencies. We thought it might be nice to spend the night at the summit.

Over a thousand people trudge to the top of Hengshan's 1,300-meter summit every day, and many of them spend the night so that they can see the sunrise the next morning. We considered joining them. But wherever we looked, we saw trash. I'm sure people congratulated themselves on reaching the summit, even if all they did was ride the bus to Nantienmen. For us, all we could feel was disappointment. It wasn't the fog or the cold. It was the garbage. We liked to think that mountains would be exempt, that they were above the red dust. But Hengshan was an exception. We headed back down.

On our way up, we had managed to avoid the road by following the trail along the mountain's western ridge. We should have returned the same way or at least taken the bus down. But the day was young, and we decided to walk. Big mistake. During previous trips, I had climbed four of China's five sacred mountains, as well as a number of scenic peaks, and I had passed through gauntlets of souvenir sellers at the country's most famous shrines and sights. But Hengshan was unique in attracting beggars, not just a few beggars, but hundreds. Nor were they your ordinary beggars; nearly all of them were missing a body part bigger than a finger. As we approached one paraplegic, he dipped one of his stumps in a bowl of red dye to give it just the right look. It was a most difficult descent, and one we were not likely to forget. We checked "climb a sacred mountain" off our list.

革命者

3. Revolutionaries

After reclaiming our gear at the bottom of the mountain, we walked out to the highway and caught the next bus heading north. It was bound for Changsha, the capital of Hunan, but we weren't going that far. Our destination was Hsiangtan, only eighty kilometers away. Since this was the main highway connecting Kuangchou and Beijing, we thought we might make Hsiangtan in an hour. We were wrong. It took

Shansi Guildhall

two and a half. The bus may have been on the main highway, but like a lot of buses in China, it stopped anytime someone waved, which was about once every minute. Fortunately, I still had a half-pint of whiskey in my bag. It was gone by the time we pulled into Hsiangtan. So was the sun. But my journal now contained this poem about our visit to China's Southern Sacred Mountain:

> *Honking buses switchback up*
> *Hengshan pilgrims walk the road*
> *past the outstretched bowls of beggars*
> *to reach the garbage pile on top*

Obviously, I was entering a dark phase and badly in need of a rosier outlook. The hotel where we spent the night didn't provide much in the way of that, but at least the water was hot enough for a bath. I'm sure we had dinner too. But if we did, I don't remember it. We were all tired from our hike up then down the mountain, and went to sleep early.

The next morning we went to see the sights of Hsiangtan, or should I say *sight*? There was only one thing we wanted to see. Hsiangtan was a town few, if any, tourists visited, much less spent the night in. The reason we were there was to see the Ch'i Pai-shih Memorial Hall. Along with Chang Ta-ch'ien (1899–1983), Ch'i Pai-shih (1864–1957) was one of China's two most famous artists of the twentieth century, and Hsiangtan was his hometown.

Unlike Chang Ta-ch'ien, who started painting seriously at the age of nine, Ch'i Pai-shih spent his early years in poverty working as a carpenter. He didn't start painting until he was twenty-seven, and his early work was far from inspiring. Then in middle age he left Hsiangtan and began traveling all over the country meeting other artists and sketching whatever he saw. But he was still a student. It wasn't until he finally settled in Beijing at the age of fifty-three that he became a painter with his own style. Suddenly he began painting with the vision of a child. He painted simple things, like cabbages and chickens and shrimps. And whatever he painted looked alive, even funny. Within a few years, he became China's most celebrated artist, and it would be hard to find a serious collection of Chinese paintings anywhere in the world that didn't include his works. What we wanted to know was, did his hometown have any?

Actually, Ch'i Pai-shih's hometown, the town where he was born, was a small farming village sixty kilometers to the east. Hsiangtan was where he grew up and lived until he was forty. Still, when we asked, no one at our hotel knew anything about a memorial hall. We thought, surely someone would have heard about something built in honor of the town's most famous resident. Indeed, someone had. We walked out to the street and started asking likely people, people who looked like they might be interested in art. A college student finally directed us down a lane that led to some vegetable fields and a large pond at the south end of town. Beside the pond were dozens of large lid-covered urns each containing a hundred or so liters of soy sauce. And next to the urns, there was a sign announcing the future home of the Ch'i Pai-shih Memorial Hall. The sign was outside a small building, and inside the building we met the future curator, T'ang Ch'ing-hai. Mister T'ang said the memorial hall wasn't due to open until the following December, assuming, he said, money could be found to build it. The building where we met him was just temporary. I heard this a lot in China in those days. Everything was planned, except the money. We asked Mister T'ang how many Ch'i Pai-shih paintings would be on display when the hall was completed, assuming the money could be found. He said he wasn't sure. It was obviously a sensitive point, and we changed the subject.

We asked Mister T'ang if he painted. He did, and he waxed poetical about it. "Painting," he said, "is like singing a song. It's like dancing. Once I start painting, I don't stop, not even for tea." We asked if we could see some of his work, and for the next hour he showed us everything he had painted for the past two years. He was no Ch'i Pai-shih, but who is? He painted with a freedom that was refreshing, mostly landscapes. He said he traveled all around China sketching. And when he got home, he painted what he had sketched.

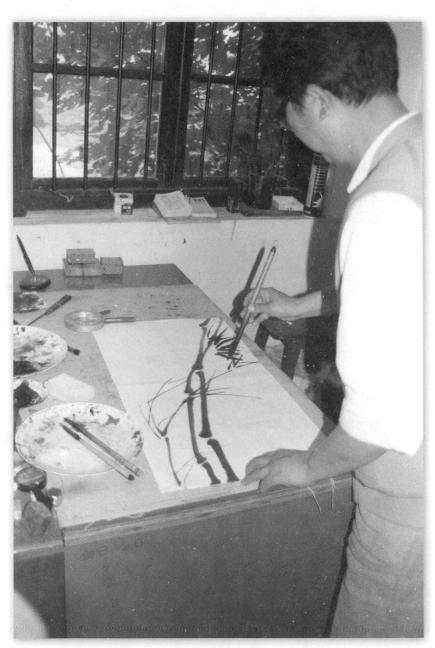

T'ang Ch'ing-hai painting

Before we said good-bye, Steve asked if he could buy one of his paintings, and Mister T'ang sold him one for 50RMB, or ten bucks. It was more of a gift than a purchase. It was a painting of a poet drinking at a place South of the Yangtze, a place we planned to visit. When we finally said good-bye, Mister T'ang asked where we were going next. We said we were going to Shaoshan. He said before we did we should visit Hsiangtan's old guildhall. Since the day was young, and we weren't in a hurry, we decided to follow his suggestion—and his directions, to the east edge of town.

Locals referred to the guildhall as Lord Kuan's Shrine because it included a shrine to Kuan-kung, the God of War. When he was alive, which was 1,800 years ago, Kuan-kung was noted for his military prowess but also for keeping his word. This last virtue endeared him to merchants, and they often built shrines to him as part of their guildhalls. This hall, though, wasn't built by the merchants of Hsiangtan but by merchants from Shansi province in North China. They hauled millet and corn to Hsiangtan and traded it for cotton and medicinal herbs, and they needed a place to conduct business negotiations as well as a place to stay. That was the function of a guildhall in China. Unfortunately, when we finally found it—which wasn't easy—it turned out to be closed.

It was already nine o'clock, so we weren't too early. Thinking there might be another entrance, we walked around the surrounding wall. No luck. We walked back to the entrance and knocked. We thought maybe someone was inside. An old man who saw us knocking said the man with the key died the day before. It wasn't our lucky day, nor the man with the key's. As we started to walk away, suddenly another man appeared, and he was holding a set of keys. Apparently, he was the new caretaker. He must have had thirty of them on a big iron ring, and being new at his job, he tried twenty-nine before the lock finally clicked and the door swung open.

The courtyard we entered was surrounded by the loveliest of gardens. It was an elegant and quiet setting, and it would have been the perfect place for people with money to conduct negotiations with other peo-

Farmhouse where Mao Tse-tung grew up

ple with money. The hall also included a huge, wonderfully wrought statue of Kuan-kung and several of the most impressive stone pillars we had seen anywhere. The old man who showed us around said the hall was first built in the Ch'ing dynasty but it was about to be renovated. He said as soon as everything was finished, the hall's ten original Ch'i Pai-shih paintings would be prominently displayed inside. We had to smile. The Ch'i Pai-shih Memorial Hall didn't have a single original by Hsiangtan's most famous artist, but the guildhall had ten. I guess only merchants could afford them.

We thanked our guide for this unexpected addition to our day, and he helped us flag down a taxi that took us back to our hotel. Once we collected our bags, we proceeded to the main bus station. Our next destination was thirty kilometers west of Hsiangtan and was the hometown of an even more illustrious son of Hunan. Ten minutes after reaching the station, we were on a bus bound for Shaoshan.

Shaoshan was where Mao Tse-tung was born, in 1893 on the day after Christmas. Mao later left this brief account of his childhood:

My family owned two and a half acres of good land, which my father had managed to buy back through small-scale trading after losing it due to debts. I began doing farm chores when I was six. We didn't eat much, but we always had enough. I started going to school when I was eight, and when I wasn't attending school I helped with the farm work. At school I read the Confucian classics, but I hated them. What I enjoyed were the historical romances, especially the stories about rebellions.

Although Mao grew up on the family farm, he had no desire to be a farmer. He saw himself in the role of a knight-errant, and when he was seventeen he left home. He didn't return home for ten years. And when he did, he didn't come back to farm. He came back to organize the local farmers and convinced his two younger brothers and his cousin to join him. Then they all went to take part in the revolution.

An hour after we left Hsiangtan, the bus dropped us off in a large public square a few kilometers west of the original village of Shaoshan. The square was in "New" Shaoshan. On one side was a guesthouse where visitors could spend the night. But we weren't planning on staying that long and walked over to the other side of the square, where there was a memorial hall and a clan hall. Sixty percent of the people living in the Shaoshan area belonged to the Mao clan, and they used the clan hall for funerals and other communal functions. The hall was also where Mao met with local farmers when he came back to win them over to the revolutionary cause.

The memorial hall next to it was built later to honor Mao. It was pretty much a waste of time. It was poorly lit and consisted mostly of documents. Some of the photos, though, were interesting, and there was an old black sedan used by Mao that was rusting along one of the corridors. We walked back to the other side of the square to where buses departed for Mao's home every fifteen minutes.

While we waited, we couldn't help noticing the mountain peak that overlooked the square to the southwest. It was called Shaofeng and was named after China's most famous ancient music, which was composed there 4,500 years ago during a visit by Emperor Shun. In Chinese, the word *shao* 韶 means "exuberant," and that was what the emperor called the music one of his officials had composed—hence the name of the peak and the town. Two thousand years later, when Confucius visited the capital of the state of Ch'i in North China, Confucius heard this music for the first time. So overwhelming was its effect on him, he didn't notice what he was eating for the next three months.

We opted to let the mountain and its music be and climbed, instead, aboard the next bus to where Mao listened to frogs and crickets and tried not to think about farming. Five minutes later, we were there. From the parking lot, we walked down a dirt road to the farmhouse where Mao grew up. The original house was destroyed by the KMT in 1929, but it had been restored to its original condition with its mud-brick walls, its dirt floor, and its thatched roof. Mao's bedroom was at the front of the building and looked out over a large pond full of lotuses left over from summer. It was a pleasant place. And it was quiet. The surrounding area was still farmland. But there wasn't much else to see, and we returned to New Shaoshan on the next bus.

Mao was certainly one of the great heroes of Chinese history. Few men accomplished as much or benefited so many. But he was also one of his country's greatest villains, and few men destroyed as much or hurt so many. I'm sure it will take a long time before the Chinese resolve their feelings about these two aspects of his legacy. Sometimes heroes live a bit too long.

Speaking of heroes, it turns out that he wasn't the only one from this area. Among his fellow revolutionaries from the same county were P'eng Te-huai (1898–1974) and Liu Shao-ch'i (1898–1969). P'eng Te-huai's hometown was thirty kilometers to the south, and Liu Shao-ch'i's was half that to the north. I suppose we could have visited the former homes of all three men in a single day, but local transportation in that area was limited and infrequent, and there weren't any taxis. So we had to choose: P'eng Te-huai or Liu Shao-ch'i.

A few years earlier, I read P'eng's autobiography *Memoirs of a Chinese Marshal*. He was the sort of man I would have liked to meet, and I asked the bus driver who plied the route between Shaoshan and Mao's home if there were any buses to P'eng's village of Wushihchen. P'eng was serving as China's Minister of Defense when he returned home in 1959. He was on his way to attend the Lushan Conference, one of the most important meetings ever held by the Communist Party, and he hadn't been to the countryside in some time. He was appalled at the poverty and starvation he saw. This was during Mao's Great Leap Forward. Following his visit, P'eng wrote an open letter blaming the suffering of the peasants directly on Mao. This was too much for the Great Helmsman. Mao stripped P'eng of his post, replaced him with Lin Piao, and purged him from the party. But that was only the beginning. Public humiliation followed public humiliation, until the Red Guards finally finished the job. P'eng died in prison, as did many others who tried to tell Mao about the sufferings he was creating. Mao's greatest failing was that he tried to model Chinese society as if he were modeling clay instead of people. If problems arose, they were the fault of the people, not the theories he was trying to implement.

The bus driver said there were no buses that went anywhere near P'eng's old village, so we turned our attention to Liu Shao-ch'i, who suffered a similar fate as P'eng. In 1966, Mao began fanning the flames of revolution again—this time a Cultural Revolution. The Chairman's Great Leap Forward had turned out to be a great leap backward, and conditions had become chaotic. Mao spotted signs of revisionism, even capitalism, and he called on the students.

Liu Shao-ch'i was president at the time, and Mao was party chairman. Liu became annoyed at Mao's attempt to destabilize an already unstable situation. He sent teams of workers onto the campuses to quell the disorder. It was then that Mao came up with one of his more memorable lines. The Chairman said, "Whoever suppresses the students will come to a bad end." I wonder if anyone in Beijing still remembers that quote.

In any case, the emperor waved his hand, and Liu was thrown to the mob. Like P'eng Te-huai, he was brutally and repeatedly humiliated in public by the Red Guards he had tried to suppress. It was too much for

Farmhouse where Liu Shao-ch'i grew up

him. Within months of being purged, Liu became ill. He already had diabetes. Now he contracted tuberculosis. When word of the former president's condition reached Mao, he ordered Liu flown from Beijing to the backwater town of Kaifeng to be treated as local conditions allowed. There were, however, no facilities capable of treating him in Kaifeng, and so Liu Shao-ch'i died soon after he landed. Another victim of the man who loved revolutions.

Liu's hometown was only fifteen kilometers northeast of Mao's, and the same bus driver said there was a bus that traveled to within a few kilometers several times a day on its way between Shaoshan and Ninghsiang. And we were in luck. The next bus left thirty minutes later with us on it. We told the driver where we wanted to go, and he let us off at a crossroads. After waiting for another thirty minutes, we caught a bus heading east, toward Changsha. Ten minutes later, we got off again just past the village of Huaminglou. After checking with the driver to make sure there would be another bus to Changsha, we walked up a side road and five hundred meters later came to the Liu Shao-ch'i Memorial Hall.

It was impressive, and new. But a little too new. The grass and plants surrounding the building looked like a bad toupee. They hadn't yet grown into the soil. But at least there were grass and plants. According to an English-language brochure, Liu Shao-ch'i was rehabilitated in 1980, two years after P'eng Te-huai—both after they had died. Previously, during the tumultuous years of the Cultural Revolution, Teng Hsiao-p'ing (1904–1997) was branded China's number-two Capitalist Roader, and Liu Shao-ch'i was number-one.

The displays inside the hall were much better than those at Mao's memorial hall. They were even interesting. They weren't all slogans and political posturing. Afterwards, we walked farther down the road to his old house. It was very similar to Mao's. Like Mao's, it also looked out across a pond where the remnants of the summer's lotuses swayed in the autumn breeze.

While we were standing there enjoying the view, we suddenly realized we were about to miss the last bus of the day. The bus driver told us the last bus to Changsha was scheduled to pass through Huaminglou at

2:30, and it was 2:30. We hurried, but it was nearly three by the time we made it to the village. We were hoping the bus was late.

We dropped our bags in the dirt next to the road and waited. Apparently no one in Huaminglou had ever seen a foreigner before, and it didn't take long for a crowd to form. When the local elementary school let out at 3:30, the crowd became a mob, and the bus was still nowhere in sight. Finally, around 4:30 the police showed up. Someone in the crowd told the police I spoke Chinese, and I cringed, regretting the day I ever learned the language. Actually, it was sort of weird, the way I learned Chinese.

After I graduated from the University of California at Santa Barbara with a degree in anthropology, I applied to Columbia University for graduate school. Since I didn't have enough money for the tuition, I checked every fellowship on the list when I applied, even one they called a "language fellowship," where applicants had to specify what language they wanted to study. I had just read a book about Zen and thought it made wonderful sense, so I wrote the word "Chinese." That was how I learned Chinese, purely by accident. And I was regretting that accident when four policemen worked their way through the crowd and pointed to a small farm shed away from the road. The officer in charge said, "Let's go talk." Of course, I didn't want to talk, especially to a policeman in a farm shed. I said, "If you want to talk, let's talk here so we can see the bus if it comes." The chief wouldn't accept this reasoning, and one of his underlings shoved his clipboard into my ribs, pushing me in the direction of the shed. Apparently, the police needed to file a report about why a crowd had formed. Instead of moving in the direction of the shed, I grabbed the policeman's wrist with one hand and with the other knocked his clipboard to the ground. Suddenly I realized I had gone too far. I had this sinking feeling. Just then, the crowd started yelling: "The bus! The bus!" Indeed, it was the bus.

As the crowd made way for the bus, we grabbed our packs then climbed aboard and waved good-bye to the good people of Huaminglou, the hometown of China's number-one Capitalist Roader. As we pulled away, the police were still standing where we had left them. They didn't wave back. They were probably wondering how they were going to fill out their report about the crowd. Crowds were actually illegal in China. Meanwhile, we yelled and laughed through the beautiful red-earth/green-field countryside of Hunan all the way to Changsha.

Changsha wasn't that far. But the bus took its time and stopped at every farm village on the way. It took over two hours to go maybe thirty kilometers. Finally, as the bus approached Changsha and was about to cross the bridge that spanned the Hsiang River, we asked the driver to let us off. The sun had already gone down, and I saw a sign for the Maple Hotel. We wanted to stay on the west side of the Hsiang, and this looked like a good spot. We thanked the driver for rescuing us at Huaminglou, waved good-bye, and walked up the hotel driveway. It looked like an oasis. But when we entered the lobby and went to the front desk, the clerk said they didn't have any rooms. It was probably our appearance. We must have looked like tramps. However, if there is one thing I have learned about staying in hotels in China, it's that there is always a room. To get that room, though, requires perseverance and good karma. Our karma, apparently, was still good. While we were standing there wondering what to do next—we hadn't seen any other hotels on the west side of the bridge, the manager passed by the front desk and saw how tired we looked, and a room suddenly materialized. And that was how we got to Changsha, on the wings of good karma.

長沙

4. Changsha

So there we were at the front desk of Changsha's Maple Hotel congratulating ourselves on getting a room. But before we headed to our room, the manager said if we wanted to eat dinner at the hotel, we would have to hurry. The restaurant stopped taking orders at eight, and it was already after seven. Usually we didn't eat in hotel restau-

Sanpan at Chutzuchou

rants; we preferred night markets or noodle stands. But the manager insisted. Since he had been instrumental in prying loose the last available room for us, we couldn't refuse. He led us into the dining room, and we ordered a couple of random dishes. Then he left, and we waited for our meal.

An hour later, we were still searching for superlatives. We had never eaten better food in China. I can still taste the crisp sesame chicken. The chef must have been trained in Heaven. And the price? Enough food and beer for the three of us cost less than 50RMB, or ten bucks. And the beer was from outside the province. The Hunan beer we drank two nights earlier tasted like formaldehyde—in fact, maybe that's what it was, left over from the recycling process.

But food and beer wasn't the reason we stayed at the Maple. It was on the west side of the Hsiang and at the foot of Yuehlushan. During our whirlwind visit of Hengyang, we visited Huiyenfeng, or Returning Goose Peak. Huiyenfeng was considered the southernmost of Hengshan's seventy-two peaks. Yuehlushan was considered its northernmost peak. And like Hengyang, it was the home of another Confucian academy, but not just any Confucian academy. It was the home of Yuehlu Academy, one of the four most famous academies in all of China. Naturally, that was our first destination the next morning.

In addition to blessing us with a hotel room and a memorable dinner, another sign that the road gods were watching over us was the presence of a bus terminus just beyond the hotel driveway. A few minutes after walking down to where buses turned around, we boarded number five. Twenty minutes later, we got off where all the students got off: at Hunan University. The academy was next to the campus, just behind the huge statue of Chairman Mao.

Ever since it was first built a thousand years ago, Yuehlu Academy was the major center of learning in the province. This was where the sons of the Hunan elite came to study. At the beginning of the twentieth century, their sons were still studying here, and it became, for a time, Hunan University. That was how most universities in China began, in the halls of Confucian academies. In the case of Hunan University, it was established in 1926. But with the development of a middle class and the need for knowledge beyond the classical education of the past, the academy wasn't big enough to contain all the students or the departments of a modern university. Hence, Hunan University was built next door.

The academy itself had been rebuilt many times, most recently in 1981, but it no longer functioned as a place of learning. It was a museum to the system of higher education that prevailed in the past. And it was in perfect condition. As we approached, we were greeted by two phrases that flanked the main entrance: "Men of talent in the land of Ch'u / this is where they bloom 惟楚有材 / 於斯為盛." The land of Ch'u was an old name for the region that included Hunan and Hupei provinces.

Inside on one of the walls was a list of eighteen rules all students were expected to follow: "think always of your parents / in all things avoid excess / let what you eat and wear be simple / act only with decorum. . ." etc. Over the entrance of the main hall were four huge characters in the calligraphy of the great neo-Confucian philosopher Chu Hsi (1130–1200), who taught here two hundred years after the academy was built. His admonition reminded students to be "loyal, filial, honest, and frugal 忠孝廉潔."

As we walked through the halls once used for instruction and the halls devoted to honoring the great Confucian sages of the past, we agreed that we would never have survived the rigor that would have been expected of us had we enrolled there. China was, after all, where bureaucracy was invented. And such academies were focused on preparing young men to fill its ranks. Serving in such a capacity required talents we didn't have and training we could never have endured. We were round pegs in a square world, or maybe it was vice versa. Yes, I would say it was vice versa. The academy was a beautiful place, but it was not for us. We turned our attention to the mountain after which it was named.

Since the day was young, we thought we would go for a hike and followed the trail that began just to the left of the academy. It was a trail of huge stone steps and sufficiently wide that we were able to walk side-by-side, which never happened in cities or towns. After only a few minutes, we paused to catch our breaths at Aiwan Pavilion. We weren't in a hurry, and the pavilion seemed like a good place to stop.

Surrounded by towering trees, lush foliage, and a lily-filled pond, it begged us to relax, and that was what we did. This was also where Mao used to relax and where he talked with his fellow students when he was studying in Changsha in the aftermath of the revolution that ended the Ch'ing dynasty. One revolution down. One more to go. The place still remembered him. In fact, the plaque announcing this as Aiwan Pavilion was written by him.

Once we had caught our breaths, we continued up the trail past Lushan Temple, which was still a functioning Buddhist monastery. We paused to catch our breaths again at the graves of Huang Hsing and Tsai Eh. Huang and Tsai were both from Changsha and played key roles in the revolution that brought the Ch'ing dynasty to an end.

When the Republic they helped established in 1912 was overthrown by Yuan Shi-k'ai, who proclaimed himself emperor of a new dynasty, Huang traveled to America and raised funds for an army, and Tsai led the army Huang funded. Tsai Eh's military successes quickly put an end to Yuan Shih-k'ai's short-lived interregnum and led to the reestablishment of the Republic in 1916. But no sooner had Huang and Tsai succeeded in overthrowing the overthrower and in reestablishing the Republic than they died, within days of each other. Their bodies were buried on Yuehlushan in a state funeral attended by hundreds of dignitaries and thousands of mourners. Mao Tse-tung, P'eng Te-huai, and Liu Shao-ch'i were not the only revolutionaries from Hunan, and I've always wondered if there wasn't something in the food. Maybe it was the red peppers. Wherever we traveled in Hunan, we saw piles of them on sidewalks and on roadsides. Revolutionary peppers.

After pausing to pay our respects to Huang and Tsai, we continued on a bit farther to a place where the trail seemed to end and where we had a grand view of the Hsiang River as it flowed northward toward the Yangtze. Beyond the Hsiang to the east, all of Changsha was spread out. It looked like it was waiting for us, and we weren't about to disappoint it. We walked back down the trail, and beneath the outstretched arm of Chairman Mao's statue we caught the number five back to the terminus near our hotel, then the number three across the Hsiang and into the heart of the city. We got off at Martyrs' Park, where the province's other revolutionaries were honored. But we weren't there to see the park. We walked north a few blocks to the entrance of the Hunan Provincial Museum.

I have since heard that the museum is now worth visiting, but we were there in 1991. We poked our heads inside but didn't spend more than half an hour. Besides, the reason we were there wasn't to visit the museum's main collection but to see the artifacts in the building next door that were unearthed from three Han dynasty tombs in a Changsha suburb.

The tombs were discovered by farmers in 1972 in the village of Mawangtui, a mere four kilometers east of the museum. The tombs were those of a local marquis, his wife, and their son, all of whom died 2,200 years ago. Earthquakes and water seepage had disturbed the clay that covered the tombs that contained the marquis and his son, but the tomb that contained the marquis's wife was more fortunate. It turns out that the ancient Chinese perfected a method of burying people that would have made the ancient Egyptians envious. They sealed a tomb with a special clay that prevented air from getting inside. But before sealing the tomb, they placed something inside the tomb that decomposed and created a gas that preserved the body of the deceased as if they had just died. Of course, the gas escaped when tombs were opened, and archaeologists have remained in the dark as to the nature of this gas.

When farmers first discovered the tombs at Mawangtui, they noticed this gas escaping through a small hole. Once researchers at the provincial museum heard about the discovery, they rushed to the site to protect it from further damage. One of the researchers was Kao Chih-hsi. When he saw the escaping gas, he tried to plug the hole and rode his bicycle back to town as fast as he could. He spent the next day pedaling all over Changsha looking for equipment to sample the gas. But this was the middle of the Cultural Revolution, and people were more interested in preserving their own positions than in helping solve secrets of China's feudal past. It took two days for Kao to obtain the necessary equipment. By the time he pedaled back to the site, the gas was gone, and its secret has remained a mystery.

Mawangtui Museum curator Kao Chih-hsi

Although the gas was gone, the body it helped to preserve was intact. Unfortunately, as soon as it came into contact with air, it began to deteriorate. Having failed to discover the mystery of the gas, Kao didn't want to lose the body too. Again, his attempts to do so were rebuffed by the authorities in Changsha. Finally, the director of the Shanghai Museum came to his aid and arranged to have a hermetically-sealed chamber constructed. The chamber worked, and the wife's skin has remained fresh to this day, even if it does look a bit ghastly. We joined other visitors in looking down at her remains. As to what killed her, researchers concluded she died from a heart attack brought on by choking on melon seeds. Melon seeds. Deadly melon seeds.

After spending 2,200 years in the ground, her body's condition was truly amazing. But even more amazing were the other contents of the tombs. First, there was the silk. In addition to the fabric used to wrap the wife's body, there were sixty-three bolts woven with the most intricate of patterns, and it was all in perfect condition. There was also a silk gown that weighed a mere forty-nine grams, or less than two ounces. It looked about as heavy as a pair of dragonfly wings.

The tombs also contained books, books copied on silk. And they weren't just any books. These were books meant to accompany the marquis and his family into the afterlife. In short, they were their favorite books. First, there were two complete copies of the most revered of all Taoist texts, the *Taoteching*. They are still the two earliest complete copies of Lao-tzu's famous text ever found, a text that he wrote a mere three hundred years earlier around 500 BC. Second, one of the copies was prefaced by four lost chapters of the *Classic of the Yellow Emperor*, China's earliest known medical treatise. A number of other texts were also found in the tombs, including the earliest known book on astronomy. Among this last book's remarkable contents were figures on the periodic motions of the planets that differed less than one-hundredth of one percent from modern estimates.

In addition to the philosophical, medical, and astronomical works, the tombs also contained maps. One of them was a remarkably accurate topographic map of most of South China, from Changsha all the way to

Kuangchou, where we began our trip. There was also a silk painting of a system of exercises designed to promote health, similar to those later developed into Taichichuan. Finally, there were paintings depicting the whole gamut of Chinese mythology, including the heavenly realm, the human realm, and the world of spirits. And, wonder of wonders, the museum's labels were also in English for people like us. One Chinese visitor at the museum told us it was his fifth visit. There was so much to see, we could have spent days. But museums can be exhausting, and after two hours we called it quits. Our eyes were glazed over.

We walked back outside and found a place to have some noodles, and wondered what else we should see in Changsha. We had the whole afternoon. Instead of more relics of the city's past, we decided on Chutzuchou (Orange Tree Island). Chutzuchou was in the middle of the Hsiang River, and the only way to reach it was to take a bus that crossed the same bridge we crossed earlier. Halfway across, however, the bus exited the bridge and drove south through the middle of the island. Chutzuchou was basically an extremely long sandbar, five kilometers long and less than two hundred meters wide. As its name suggested, it was once famous for its orange trees, and we passed thousands as we drove toward the upriver end of the island.

There were a number of small villages on the island, and our bus was filled with villagers heading back home after a morning in town. It was slow going, but finally we reached the end of the line. The driver told us buses departed every hour or so. As far as we were concerned, that was perfect. We were in no hurry. There was a small park and a sandy beach at the end of the island. The place was doubtlessly packed in summer, but we were here in early October and found ourselves nearly alone. Just us and a couple of fishermen and their small skiffs.

We sat down on the sand and for the next two hours did nothing at all—well, we did catch up on our journals, but it seemed like nothing at all. At some point, one of the fishermen came over to where we were lounging and offered to take us out on the river. He said we could go fishing. But we weren't interested in fishing. We were busy doing nothing, just staring at the Hsiang's passing current and the distant peaks of

Hengshan and writing in our journals. We weren't the only ones who sat here doing just that. Tu Fu (712–770) came here the year he died. It was his second spring in a row in Changsha, and as he lay ill inside the small boat that served as his home, he wrote "Written on My Boat When Swallows Come":

> *A traveler in Hunan in the middle of spring*
> *two years now I've watched swallows carrying mud*
> *in my garden back home we were friends*
> *here they regard me from a distance*
> *the poor things nesting wherever they can*
> *no different from this homeless life of mine*
> *they chirp from the mast then fly off*
> *while my handkerchief only gets damper*

The boats pulled up on the shore where we were sitting were *sanpans*. They were called *sanpans* because their hulls were originally made of three (*san*) boards (*pan*), one for the bottom and two for the sides. I'm guessing Tu Fu's boat was bigger, probably a five-board *wupan* with a mast and a covered shelter.

Tu Fu lived at the height of the golden age of Chinese poetry. In fact, he was the height. He was born in the hills east of the eastern capital of Loyang, but he spent most of his life in the hills south of the western capital of Ch'ang-an. Despite his fame as a poet, he held only a few minor posts and fell out of favor during the aftermath of the An Lu-shan Rebellion (755–759), when both capitals lay in ruins and bandits roamed the countryside. After lying low with his family in Szechuan and later in the Yangtze Gorges, he sailed his little boat down the Yangtze and spent his last two years following the Hsiang River upstream, past Changsha and Hsiangtan, and even as far as Hengyang. On his way back downstream, he died near the town of Yuehyang just south of where the Hsiang joins the Yangtze. He was fifty-nine, and the first frost had already fallen. This is how he ended one of his last poems:

For ten-thousand miles on earth and in heaven
I can't find a place of my own
my wife and children are still with me
whenever I see them I sigh
the country is a wasteland of weeds
my friends and neighbors are gone
where is the way back home
my tears fall on the banks of the Hsiang

It was hard to imagine: China's greatest poet, adrift, in his little boat with his wife and children, a thousand miles from home, going from one moorage to the next. Earlier, when we were at the Hunan Museum that afternoon, I asked several officials who worked there about the location of Tu Fu's grave. I also asked at the travel service in our hotel that morning. All I got were blank stares. No one I asked had heard of his grave, much less knew where it was. We wouldn't have tried to find it ourselves, but I had an old map of the province, and Tu Fu's grave was a small dot on it, a dot about a hundred kilometers northeast of Changsha. It looked like it was in the middle of nowhere. But nowhere had never stopped us before.

5. Poets

The next morning, after checking out of our beloved Maple Hotel, we took a taxi to the main bus station. The closest town to the dot on my map was Anting. From Changsha, there were two buses a day, one at 7:30 and another at 1:30. We were in luck. We arrived just minutes before the 7:30 left. We even got seats. Three hours later, we were there, in Anting, or as the bus driver called it: Kuantang.

Ch'u Yuan Shrine relief

As the bus continued on, we found ourselves standing at the edge of a very crowded street. It was market day. But while we were standing there wondering what to do next, people stopped buying and selling whatever it was they were buying and selling. The word *wai-kuo-jen*, or "foreigner," spread through the crowd like a fire across the prairie. Suddenly we were more interesting than market day.

When the crowd around us became sufficiently large, I announced to no one in particular that we were looking for Tu Fu's grave. Blank looks all around. Was my map wrong? Word spread, though, and before long a man worked his way through the crowd and said he knew where the grave was located and for 30RMB, or six bucks, he would take us there on his tractor. The price was a little steep for a ride on a tractor, but Tu Fu rated as much respect as we could muster, and we agreed.

From Kuantang, or Anting—take your pick—we headed west on the highway that led to Pingchiang. After about three kilometers, we turned south onto a dirt road. Actually, it wasn't a road. It was a pair of ruts, and we followed them south another four or five kilometers through rice fields and across hills planted with tea bushes and tea-oil trees (*Camellia oleifera*). Actually, we weren't on the farmer's tractor. We were standing in the carryall he was pulling behind his tractor.

It was a rough road and our hands hurt from trying to hang onto the metal railing. Finally, after about twenty minutes of careening along, the farmer pulled into a flat grassy area next to a long white wall. He said we were here. We didn't know what to expect, but we were expecting something different. The shrine built in honor of Tu Fu centuries ago had become the local elementary school. As our tractor pulled up outside the entrance, the principal came outside to see what a tractor was doing there. We waved, and he waved back. When we got off and explained the purpose of our visit, he led us inside. There was a portrait of Tu Fu off to one side. But over the entryway in the place of honor were portraits of Marx, Lenin, Mao, and Stalin. Even at his own grave, Tu Fu got second billing. The portrait of Stalin was especially noteworthy, as this was 1991. Mao denounced the Russian version of Communism in 1961, and relations between the two countries weren't

Tu Fu's grave

normalized again until 1989, only two years before we walked past Stalin's portrait. Either word traveled very slowly in the Hunan countryside, or it traveled very quickly.

After passing beneath the heroes of Communism, we followed the principal down several corridors past the third- then the fourth-grade classrooms. At the end of one of the corridors, he unlocked a gate that led to a weed-filled enclosure. At the back of the walled-in enclosure was Tu Fu's grave: his grass-covered mound was surrounded by a wall of stones, and there was a stone tablet in front with his name on it. Among the weeds, we spotted a marijuana plant but made no attempt to harvest its buds. While we were standing there, the whole school—students and teachers—came out to watch us. Apparently, our presence was too disruptive to try to maintain order. We paid our respects as best we could with the traditional three bows, then thanked the principal and returned to our tractor. By the time we left, it was noon, when the children normally went home for lunch. As our tractor pulled away, more than a hundred children chased our carryall. Several of them even managed to grab hold of the railing and climb inside. As we passed their houses, one by one they jumped off, then stood there waving until we disappeared.

When we finally reached the highway, instead of heading east back to Anting, we asked our driver if he would take us west to Pingchiang. It was another six or seven kilometers down the road and in the direction we wanted to go, and we saw no sense in going back to Anting. Naturally, we offered to double the farmer's fare. He agreed, and off we went. It was a beautiful day, and the highway was paved. We felt blessed to be riding in the open with the wind blowing through our hair and the sun shining down on us. Thirty minutes later, we climbed off at the Pingchiang bus station. And thirty minutes after that, we were on a bus. As we rolled along to the next place on our itinerary, I wrote another poem. It was called "Visiting Tu Fu's Grave with Finn and Steve":

> *On a rolling red clay hill*
> *covered with oil-nut trees*

miles from the nearest town
we stopped at a dirt-floor school

On a rolling red clay hill
surrounded by terraced rice
next to the fourth grade class
we entered a garden of weeds

On a rolling red clay hill
we stood and bowed three times
at a place called Little Heaven
in front of Tu Fu's grave

On a rolling red clay hill
the principal waved good-bye
and a hundred children chased us
where a stranger stopped to die

It didn't seem as dark as my last poem. It must have been the sunshine. From Pingchiang the road followed the Milo River downstream through a countryside of farms and forested hills. Seventy kilometers and two and a half hours later, our bus pulled into the town named for the river. Outside the bus station, we flagged down a taxi and told the driver to take us to a hotel. It turned out there was only one hotel in Milo that accepted foreigners. We had no choice but to check into the Milo City Government Reception Center. It was quiet, the rooms were decent enough, and the price was reasonable: only 30RMB, or $6, for a triple.

From our balcony, we watched the sun go down then went to find a place to eat. On our way out, we stopped to talk with the manager, and he suggested we eat at the reception center restaurant. After our dining experience at the Maple Hotel in Changsha, we had changed our opinion about hotel restaurants. An hour later, the old opinion was back. Even now, I feel queasy just thinking about that meal. It floated in oil, and not the good kind of oil. And they charged as much as the Maple Hotel. It was my fault, though. They didn't have a printed menu, and I made the mistake of ordering without asking the prices. After dinner, I told the manager we would skip breakfast.

But before we headed back to our rooms, I thought I would enlist his help in arranging our transportation for the following day. Our next destination was another middle-of-nowhere poet's grave. I knew there wouldn't be any buses, so I asked if he could arrange for someone to take us there. An hour later, he knocked on our door and said he had found a driver. The price, he said, would be 100RMB. Since we really didn't have a choice, I told him that would be fine. Fortunately, the water was hot enough for a bath that night, and we went to bed happy.

When we checked out the next morning, the driver was waiting. And he was waiting beside a car, not a tractor. The manager was waiting too. He wanted to make sure we got off okay. We thanked him for helping make the arrangements, and he assured us that the driver knew where we wanted to go—which was good, because our destination was once more just a dot on my map. We put our bags in the trunk and were off. A few minutes later, the town of Milo was behind us and we began driving west along the Milo River again.

It was along this river that the first dragon boat races took place over 2,000 years ago. The races began in honor of Ch'u Yuan (343–278 BC), China's first great poet. Ch'u Yuan grew up in the Yangtze Gorges, where for generations his family had served the state of Ch'u as Lords of the Gorges. That was during the fourth century BC, when a number of states were attempting to unify all of China under their rule. When Ch'u Yuan criticized his ruler for believing the false promises of the state of Ch'in, his ruler banished him. This occurred in 296 BC, and Ch'u Yuan tells the story in one of his own poems, a poem entitled "The Fisherman":

When Ch'u Yuan was banished
he wandered along rivers
he sang on their banks
weak and forlorn

till a fisherman asked
aren't you Lord of the Gorges
what fate has brought you to this?

Ch'u Yuan answered
the world is muddy
I alone am clean
everyone's drunk
I alone am sober
and so they sent me away.

The fisherman said
a sage isn't bothered by others
he can change with the times
if the world is muddy
splash in the mire
if everyone's drunk
drink up the dregs
why get banished
for deep thought and purpose?

Ch'u Yuan said he had heard
when you clean your hair
you should dust off your hat
when you take a bath
you should shake out your robe
how can I let something so pure
be ruined and wronged by others
I'd rather jump into the Hsiang
and be buried in a fish's gut
than let something so white
be stained by common dirt.

The fisherman smiled and rowed away singing
"When the river is clear I wash my hat
when the river is muddy I wash my feet."
And once gone he was heard from no more.

Not long after Ch'u Yuan poked fun at himself in this poem, he heard the news that the state of Ch'in had finally conquered Ch'u, as he had feared it would. He was so disconsolate that he took his own advice and jumped into the Milo not far from where it flowed into the Hsiang.

We followed the river he jumped into more than ten kilometers on a dike road that ran along the river's southern embankment. Dotting the grass-covered flood plain were water buffaloes and herds of goats and flocks of ducks and geese. It was such a rare scene in China, to see so much verdant land and no villages, no buildings, no people other than the occasional fisherman casting his net. After about thirty minutes, we pulled up behind half a dozen vehicles waiting at the Chutang Ferry. The boat we all were waiting for was a metal-hulled barge with an engine that pulled itself across the river on a cable. The river wasn't more than two hundred meters wide at this point, and we only had to wait twenty minutes before it was our turn. Once we were on the other side, we followed a side road on the right to a nearby promontory that overlooked the river. This was what we were looking for: the site of the Ch'u Yuan Shrine.

While he pondered his future, this was where Ch'u Yuan lived, on a small hill beside the river. According to the shrine's caretaker, the spot where Ch'u Yuan drowned was seven kilometers farther downstream. He said there used to be a shrine there too, but it was destroyed by the Red Guards. He said most of the people who visited the shrine at the Chutang Ferry were Japanese. That surprised us. But what really surprised us was the reason. He said a scholar in Japan had written a book in which he claimed Ch'u Yuan was, believe it or not, Japanese. Give a scholar a couple of facts and enough rope, and he'll either tie them together or hang himself trying.

As for the shrine near the ferry, it had been here since the Han dynasty, or nearly 2,000 years. The current version dated from the eighteenth century and included an unusually realistic relief above the entrance showing Ch'u Yuan standing among the waves. The halls reminded us of those at the Yuehlu Academy in Changsha: exposed timbers and whitewashed walls covered with scrolls featuring the calligraphy of famous visitors. Clearly, Ch'u Yuan had not been forgotten.

When we told the caretaker that we were poets ourselves—and no one was there to say we weren't—he invited us to stay for tea. One of the questions we asked while we were waiting for the tea to cool was whether Ch'u Yuan's body was ever recovered and if so where his grave was located. The caretaker said the body was, indeed, recovered but Ch'u Yuan didn't have just one grave, he had twelve, and they were spread across the countryside between the Chutang Ferry and the town of Milo. He said the reason there were so many was to discourage grave robbers. When we asked if he had a favorite, he said he liked number four near the railway bridge just north of town.

Whether or not Ch'u Yuan's body was actually recovered, a whole festival grew up around his death. In English it's known as the Dragon Boat Festival, because of the custom of racing boats to see who can reach Ch'u Yuan's body before the water dragons do. In Chinese, it's called Tuanwuchieh, the Festival of the Midday Sun, because it's celebrated on the fifth day of the fifth month, which occurs within a few days of the summer solstice when the sun is at its height. It's one of China's oldest festivals, and it has been associated with Ch'u Yuan for nearly 2,000 years. Nowadays it's also celebrated as Poets' Day.

While we sipped our tea, the caretaker told us about all the sites in the area associated with Ch'u Yuan slated for development. Big plans were afoot. I had to wonder where he expected the tourists, much less the money, to come from. According to the guest register we signed when we first arrived, the shrine didn't get more than a dozen people a month. Still, we were glad to know that the authorities had not forgotten Ch'u Yuan. One of our favorite poets was Wang Wei (699–759), and Wang Wei said he never traveled anywhere without a copy of Ch'u Yuan's poems. Ch'u Yuan's sense of diction and rhythm became the model cultivated by all of China's great poets.

Ch'u Yuan grave #4

Finally, we thanked our host and returned to Milo. But on the way, we asked our driver to take us by the grave just north of town near the railway bridge. It wasn't easy to find, but our driver kept asking, and farmers kept pointing. Finally we found it: a weed-covered mound and a tombstone with the words "Grave of Ch'u Yuan, Lord of the Three Gorges."

We stopped long enough to pay our respects, then continued into town. As we reached the highway, we asked our driver to stop. We saw no reason to drive into town to catch a bus when we could catch one on the highway. After getting our bags out of his trunk, we stood there waiting for the next bus heading north. It was a short wait. And as we rattled toward our next destination, I wrote yet another poem—maybe I was a poet. That made three. I titled this one "Visiting the Lord of the Gorges":

> *His grave is near the railroad bridge*
> *his shrine overlooks the Chutang Ferry*
> *the caretaker poured us cups of tea*
> *still fragrant after all these years*

江上之神

6. The Spirit of the River

Ninety minutes after leaving Milo, we arrived in the town of Yueh-yang on the east shore of Tungting Lake and at the northern border of Hunan. Hunan means "south of the lake," and Tungting is the lake. It's China's second largest freshwater lake, and its major tributary is the Hsiang, which we'd been following since we arrived in the prov-

Yuehyanglou

ince. The lake, in turn, empties into the Yangtze, just a few kilometers north of Yuehyang. In fact, Yuehyang is actually a Yangtze River port.

From the bus station, we walked down the main street toward the lake and checked into a hotel that overlooked its wide waters. It was late afternoon, but there was still plenty of daylight left. So we walked back outside and down the street that ran parallel to the lake. We wanted to watch the sunset at the city's main attraction: Yuehyang Tower. China had three such towers dating back nearly two thousand years. The other two were in Wuhan and Nanchang. The one in Yuehyang was the smallest of the three. It was only fifteen meters high. But it was a better place to watch the sunset than the other two, both of which now look out over polluted cities.

From the balcony that circled its second story, we watched the lake turn gold then red then pink then finally purple. This is why the tower was built here in the first place—not to watch sunsets, but to watch the lake. It was built as an observation platform from which to monitor naval maneuvers. That was nearly 1,800 years ago, and it's been rebuilt several times since then, each time in a different form. Most recently it was restored to look as it did in the Sung dynasty, a thousand years ago, with a series of roofs that look as if they might take off with the rest of the building.

After watching the sky merge with the lake, we walked back to our hotel along the promenade that skirted the shore. Like all the lakes along the Yangtze, it serves the purpose of flood control and varies in size throughout the year, ranging anywhere from 3,000 square kilometers in winter to 20,000 in summer. During winter, the average depth drops to less than three meters, making boats largely useless. In fact, during winter many of the lake's islands can be reached by bicycle or even car. We were there at the end of September, and boats were still operating twice a day to the island whose black outline rose ever so slightly above the horizon. It was the lake's most famous island: Chunshan. And it was our destination the next morning.

We got up just in time to catch the 7:30 boat. There were only four boats a day, and ours was as packed as any bus we had been on. We wondered if perhaps the number of passengers exceeded the boat's capacity. But I suppose it didn't matter. The lake was shallower than your average swimming pool. If the boat sank, I don't think anyone would have drowned.

Just before casting off, the captain invited us up to the wheelhouse, and we watched him navigate through a course of bamboo poles that marked the way to the island. He said it was the only route deep enough for his boat. He said the days of Tungting Lake were numbered. Every year it filled up with more and more silt from excessive logging and tea terracing along its tributaries.

Actually, tea was one of the reasons we wanted to go to Chunshan. Its slopes produced one of the finest teas in China. It was called Maochien, or Fur Tip, because it was picked while the leaves were still enclosed in their furry casings, before they unfurled and started manufacturing chlorophyll and caffeine. Hence, it was a white tea, not a green tea. The best variety was called Yinchen, or Silver Needle. Unfortunately, it was only available in spring, and we were here in fall. Second best, though, wasn't bad. As soon as we arrived, we walked over to a café and ordered some. While we sat there, waiting for our tea to brew, the leaves hung in our glasses, like hundreds of miniature knives, still encased in their sheaths. Eventually, the leaves began to settle, and we tasted it. It tasted like the morning dew.

But Chunshan Island was famous for something other than tea. It was also famous for a pair of graves that date back 4,200 years to the time of Emperor Shun. The graves are those of the emperor's two wives. When Emperor Yao chose Shun to succeed him, he gave Shun his two daughters in marriage, and they rarely left his side. After ruling China for more than thirty years, Shun decided to inspect the uncivilized regions to the south of his empire. He left his wives where the Hsiang empties into Tungting Lake, while he crossed the mountains south of Hengyang into what is now Kuangsi province. Unfortunately, the natives did not welcome his visit, and Emperor Shun died in a battle just outside Wuchou, the same Wuchou tourists pass through nowadays on their way from Kuangchou to the miniature mountains of Kueilin.

When word of their husband's death reached Shun's wives, they drowned themselves in the Hsiang, and their bodies were buried on Chunshan. Once we finished our tea, we walked over to their graves and to the shrine built in their honor. Among the *Nine Elegies* attributed to Ch'u Yuan was one dedicated to them that he titled "Ladies of the Hsiang." It began:

> *Come down, royal maidens, to this northern isle*
> *pity me with your gaze*
> *the wind of autumn stirs*
> *waves on Tungting and falling leaves*
> *and me looking past the flowering sedge*
> *to an evening planned with my lover . . .*

What was there about the Hsiang that pulled China's poets and lovers into its waters? It wasn't a question for which I had an answer.

After paying our respects, we walked around the island—it was sufficiently small that it only took an hour. We returned to Yuehyang on the same boat and checked out of our hotel. A taxi took us to the train station, and the next local took us north. As usual, there weren't any seats. But when the conductor passed through checking tickets, he took pity on us and led us to a sleeper at the front of the train. It was early afternoon and most of the bunks were empty. It was such a rare treat that we stretched out and slept. Three hours later, the conductor woke us in time to get off at the town of Puchi.

Puchi was also known as Chihpi City. Either way, it wasn't our destination. But the day was sufficiently late, and there were no more buses to where we wanted to go—which was the Yangtze. We walked a few blocks from the station and checked into the only hotel that accepted foreigners. It wasn't a memorable night. But at least we were making progress. We were now in Hupei province, *hu-pei* meaning "north of the lake." We had finally left the suicidal waters of the Hsiang and Tungting Lake behind.

The next morning we went to say hello to the Yangtze into which they drained. From Chihpi City, we took the eight o'clock bus bound for Hunghu, which was on the other side of the river. An hour later, the driver dropped us off in Chihpi Township, which was little more than a village. The bus, meanwhile, continued on to the ferry that conveyed people and vehicles to the north side of the river.

The Yangtze was only a kilometer away, but we didn't feel like walking that far with our bags and stashed them at a dry goods store before heading off. We walked about twenty minutes along a dirt road until it ended at an embankment that overlooked the waters of the river the Chinese call the Long River. During the summer, the Yangtze carries more water than any other river in the world. But we were there in fall, and the river had shrunk to less than a kilometer across. After standing there watching boats of every size chug past, we continued along a dirt path that followed the embankment to a promontory that jutted into the river. A few minutes later, we were standing on the cliff that was the scene of the most famous battle ever fought in China. The name of the place was Chihpi, or Red Cliff, a name it shared with the village where we stashed our bags and the city where we spent the night.

The battle was fought here in 208 AD. The Han dynasty had come to an end a few years earlier, and the empire had split into two competing powers. Their forces faced each other where we were standing. The northern forces were commanded by Ts'ao Ts'ao, one of the most famous political and military figures in Chinese history. But the chief advisor of the southern forces was the most famous Chinese military strategist who ever lived. His name was Chu-ko Liang. Once, in broad daylight, he drove off a force of 200,000 with fewer than 2,000 soldiers. On another occasion, he repelled an entire army by playing his zither atop a city wall. This time he was outnumbered again, and once more he rose to the occasion.

Not only was Chu-ko Liang a great strategist, he was also conversant with the Ways of Heaven. There may have been more momentous battles in Chinese history, but this was and remains the most famous. The reason for its fame derives largely from its portrayal in a Ming dynasty historical novel known as *The Romance of the Three Kingdoms*. Writing about his childhood, Mao Tse-tung remembered, "Among my classmates, this was our favorite book. We knew its stories by heart."

The novel described in wonderful detail how Chu-ko Liang built a tower above Red Cliff and asked Heaven for wind. He needed the wind to carry light boats full of straw, sulfur, saltpeter, and fish oil across the Yangtze into the anchored ships of the northern forces. The wind came on cue, the straw was ignited, and the forces of the north were destroyed. As we stood there at the edge of Red Cliff looking out on the river where these events took place, we thought back to two years earlier when we visited the Chu-ko Liang shrine at the foot of the Chungnan Mountains west of Sian where he died. In the shrine's courtyard, we ran our hands across a meteorite that fell nearby the day he died. It felt as smooth as a tear.

After lingering at Red Cliff for an hour, we walked back to the village where we got off the bus earlier and collected our bags. There weren't many buses that plied that route, but an hour later the same bus came back through on its way back to Puchi. Once the bus reached the end of the line, we got out and began walking to the town's other bus station. Lots of towns in China have several stations, and Puchi had two. The bus driver said the last bus of the day to our next destination was due to leave from the other station in thirty minutes, and it was a ten-minute walk. That should have posed no problem, but halfway there I discovered my journal was missing. Apparently I dropped it on the bus that brought us back from the river. We ran back to the terminal, and I found the bus in the parking lot, but my journal was nowhere in sight. My journal contained my notes, my insights, my witticisms—in a word, my job.

While I was standing there wondering what to do, a lady selling popsicles to the people boarding other buses came up to me and asked if I had lost something. I sighed and told her I had lost my journal. She said she saw someone pick something up off the floor of the bus. My heart jumped at the thought of getting my journal back, but I was running out of time. I had another bus to catch. I told her if she could find the person, I would gladly pay her for her effort. Then the strangest thing happened. She asked me how much I would be willing to pay, then opened the lid of her ice chest just enough so that I could see my journal

Red Cliff

inside. After a brief negotiation, I ransomed my journal, and my job, for 15RMB, or $3. Finn and Steve and I then ran as fast as we could and caught the last bus of the day to Wuhan, just as it was pulling out of the station. We spent the next three hours trying to catch our breaths.

Just as the sun was setting, we arrived in Wuchang, the oldest and largest of three cities that make up Wuhan. The *wu* in Wuhan came from Wuchang, on the south shore of the Yangtze. The *han* came from the two cities of Hankou and Hanyang on the north shore. Their *han* in turn came from the Han River, which flows between the two before entering the Yangtze.

Until a hundred years ago, Hankou was hardly more than a ferry crossing and Hanyang barely a town. Wuchang was the center of government administration and commerce in this part of China and had been for over two thousand years. Ironically, Wuchang was also where traditional China ended and modern China began. In 1911, a garrison of army engineers stationed here staged the revolt that sparked the revolution that led to the end of 5,000 years of imperial rule and the founding of the Republic.

Although Wuchang is the center of what was happening in Wuhan, we had other plans. We wanted to stay on the other side of the Yangtze. Also, we had this image of going to sleep next to the river. We piled into a taxi and asked the driver to recommend a hotel that fit our imagination. Unfortunately, he shared the opinion of most taxi drivers in China that foreigners are wealthy. He drove us to the towering Chingchuan Hotel in Hanyang. We were too tired to argue with his choice, but we couldn't help feeling out of place walking into the marble-lined lobby. We felt even more out of place when the desk clerk told us rooms cost 170RMB, or $35. Normally we avoided such hotels. But every once in a while we liked to indulge ourselves with a little opulence. Besides, we figured we had been saving money by staying in government reception centers and guesthouses and it was time to splurge. And that was what we did. From our room on the fourteenth floor, we had an incredible view of the Yangtze and the bridge across it that Mao helped build. We felt wealthy.

Once we took in the luxury to which we had committed ourselves, we went back down to the ground floor and had an equally luxurious dinner in a restaurant across the street. We felt like we were on vacation. We even had a bottle of wine with our meal. In fact, we not only had a bottle with our meal, we bought four more bottles in the hotel convenience store and took them up to our room. We pulled all three chairs in the room up to the window and took in the view of Wuchang's twinkling lights and the black ribbon of the river. We watched the show until the wine was gone, all four bottles. It was three o'clock when we finally went to bed. We were definitely on vacation.

The next morning didn't happen, at least not for us. We tried to get up early but gave up. We slept until eleven. Even then, it was a struggle. But it was time to check out, and we had no choice. Still, we didn't go far. We took a taxi to Hanyang's Ancient Zither Terrace and were there in five minutes. After leaving our bags at the entrance, we walked up the steps to the top of the terrace where Yu Po-ya met Chung Tzu-ch'i.

Yu Po-ya was one of ancient China's most famous musicians, but he never felt his music was truly appreciated until the day he met Chung Tzu-ch'i. One day around 1000 BC, when Po-ya was playing his zither on this very terrace overlooking the place where the Han River joins the Yangtze, a wood collector stopped to listen. The wood collector's name was Chung Tzu-ch'i. When Po-ya was done playing, Tzu-ch'i described to Po-ya what the musician had been thinking about while he played. Po-ya was so impressed the two became fast friends despite belonging to very different social classes. Years later, when Chung Tzu-ch'i died, Yu Po-ya smashed his zither and never played again. Why play when no one understands? Ever since then, the Chinese have used their example to refer to a friend who truly understands the other. They call such a person a *chih-yin*, someone who "knows your tune."

We sat there in the shade of some ancient gingkos. We, too, knew what the other was thinking: that we had too much to drink the night before, that we should have gone to sleep earlier, but that at least we didn't hurt anyone or break anything. It wasn't much, but it was good enough for us. After sitting in the shade watching the wind blow a few thousand leaves from the gingkos surrounding the terrace, we decided it was time to get on with the day.

We returned to the park entrance, collected our bags, and took a taxi across the Han River to the Hankou pier. Hankou was where boats departed that traveled along the Yangtze, and our next destination was downriver. We bought three tickets for the evening boat to Chiuchiang. There was only one boat a day, and it didn't leave until eight o'clock that night, which left us with six hours to kill. We decided to keep moving. We left our bags in the luggage depository at the pier and took the ferry that operated between Hankou and Wuchang. On the other side, there were buses waiting for passengers exiting the ferry, and one of them took us to the Hupei Provincial Museum.

Like Changsha's Mawangtui Museum, it was the beneficiary of recent archaeological excavations, in particular the excavation of a tomb belonging to a marquis who lived slightly earlier than his fellow marquis buried at Mawangtui. This particular tomb was discovered 150 kilometers northwest of Wuhan in 1978 near the town of Suichou. Altogether some 15,000 objects were unearthed, and more than a thousand of those were on exhibit in the museum. They were the personal belongings of Marquis Yi of Tseng, or Tseng Hou-yi, who died in 430 BC. I had heard about the collection, but I had no idea it was so awesome. The artistry was truly beyond compare. I had never seen anything like it. These weren't simply objects found in the ground. Each and every object was a museum piece, a piece worthy of a pedestal. I could list dozens, but my favorite was a life-size bronze animal that combined the body of a crane and the antlers of a deer, two recurring symbols of immortality. Any sculptor alive would be envious.

The marquis's inner and outer coffins were also impressive. Weighing an incredible nine tons, they were constructed with frameworks of bronze and inlaid with rare woods that were then lacquered and painted with artistic motifs. But the marquis didn't limit himself to taking his belongings with him into the Great Beyond, he took his women too, over twenty of them. After examining their remains, scientists determined that the women ranged in age from thirteen to twenty-six and that they all were poisoned.

Aside from its more heartbreaking contents, the tomb also contained the single most important collection of bronzes ever found in China. In ancient China the production of bronze was primarily intended for ritual communication with the spiritual realm and only secondarily for warfare. The importance of the collection uncovered in the marquis's tomb was that it spanned the whole gamut of ritual usage and also revealed a consistent artistic vision of one cultural area at one point in time. It was its own museum.

While we were viewing this incredible collection, we heard music coming down one of the corridors and went to investigate. In one of the halls, a woman was playing a set of several dozen bronze bells found inside the tomb. The sound was so deep and so resonant we felt our heads reverberating, as each bell kept ringing long after the next one was struck. When the woman was done, she said that Chinese art historians considered the set of bells unearthed in the tomb the finest part of the entire collection, which was saying a lot.

There was so much to see, but our attention span was fading. After an hour, we called it quits and walked back out onto the road and caught another bus. We got off short of the Yangtze River Bridge at Huangholou, or Yellow Crane Tower. This was the second of China's three ancient towers. Unlike its counterpart in Yuehyang, it had been rebuilt out of cement instead of wood. Somehow the cement seemed more appropriate. Standing fifty meters high, the tower was the symbol of one of China's major industrial centers, and its upper balconies provided a good view of the Yangtze as it flowed past a horizon of smokestacks. The tower's name came from the crane that carried a Taoist immortal to paradise from that very spot two thousand years ago. We settled for a taxi back to the ship we hoped would carry us to dreamland and a good night's sleep.

We weren't immortals, and the River Spirit #5 wasn't a yellow crane, but it left Hankou at eight o'clock with us on it. We even had beds, albeit in adjacent cabins. The passenger ships that ply the Yangtze have four classes of accommodation: fifth-class amounts to one large room

Yellow Crane Tower

with fifty bunks, fourth-class cabins have a dozen bunks, third-class has six bunks and second-class has two bunks and a wash basin. On our boat there was no first-class. We decided to splurge and bought second-class tickets at a cost of 90RMB, or about $18, per person for the 270-kilometer voyage to Chiuchiang.

After eating dinner near the pier, we boarded thirty minutes before sailing. We should have boarded earlier. We were too late to get cabins along the outside railing and had to settle for two on the inside corridor. Passengers, we discovered later, were allowed to board one hour before sailing, and the choice of cabins was on a first-come, first-served basis. That could have been important if we had been traveling on a hot summer night. It was late fall. Still, it was boring sitting inside our cabins looking at the walls. As soon as the ship's staff retired for the night, we grabbed our blankets and pillows and lay down on the foredeck with a dozen bottles of beer. There was a good breeze, and the River Spirit was flying down the Yangtze.

About halfway through our beer supply, we wondered how fast we were going and decided to ask. We wandered up to the top deck and knocked on a door. There wasn't a sign, but Steve had worked on enough boats to know the door led to the wheelhouse. We opened it and entered a room that could have held a hundred bunks, but it was completely empty. And it was completely dark, except for the glow of a compass and a radar screen and their reflection in the faces of the captain and the first mate.

The wheelhouse was like the cockpit of an airplane, and visitors were not usually welcome. But the captain waved for us to join him. The question that prompted our excursion was the ship's speed, and that turned out to be a respectable thirty kilometers an hour. Except for the occasional running light from a passing coal barge or container ship, the river was dark. So was the sky. It had clouded over. The first mate took out his flashlight and showed us where we were on the map. As soon as he said the name, we thanked him and hurried back to our beer supply. We didn't want to pass by the place without toasting one of China's most famous poets.

The name of the place we were passing was Chihpi, or Red Cliff. There were two places on the Yangtze with that name. We had already visited one of them two hundred kilometers upriver from Wuhan, where China's most famous battle was fought in 208 AD. One hundred kilometers downriver from Wuhan, there was another Red Cliff. This one was where a poet rowed out into the Yangtze with several friends and a jug of wine one night in 1082. The poet's name was Su Tung-p'o, and he wrote two of his most famous poems there: his "Red Cliff Odes." In the first poem, he lamented the impermanence of the ever-flowing river and the ever-changing moon, then laughed in praise of their inexhaustible presence. In the second, he fell asleep drunk only to wake and look in vain for the crane that had flown above him in his dream, then transformed itself into a Taoist immortal. After toasting Su, we, too, fell asleep. But we remained in the land of mortals. Sometime after midnight, the rain woke us up and forced us back into our cabins. We went back to sleep, but not for long.

盧山

7. Lushan

A blast from the ship's horn woke us up at 4:30. We had arrived in Chiuchiang. Still half-asleep, we staggered off the ship with our rucksacks. Suddenly, we woke up. It was pouring. Fortunately, there were dozens of taxis and minivans waiting to meet passengers. While we stood there getting soaked listening to drivers listing options and fares,

Lushan's eastern flank on a rare clear day

we saw some of our fellow passengers filing into a tour bus. It was the all-day tour of nearby Lushan. We didn't really have a plan and couldn't think of anything better, so we decided to join them.

Lushan is one of China's most scenic mountains. It is especially famous for its fog-shrouded peaks and waterfalls. Tourists have been coming to Lushan for more than 1,500 years, but the road to the long, flat top of the mountain wasn't completed until 1953. Since then, Lushan has become one of the country's most popular destinations, and I suppose we should have been thankful for the rain. Except for our fellow passengers on the tour bus, we found ourselves alone on the mountain. Of course, there was a reason why we were alone. Every time the bus stopped, and the guide led us to some spot to see another fog-shrouded pinnacle or waterfall, we were drenched by the rain. When it became obvious that the rain wasn't going to stop, we left the bus when it stopped to let people use a public toilet. Looming in the fog ahead, we saw the Lulin Hotel and hurried there as fast as we could.

The Lulin was an old hotel, with stone walls and wooden floors, and we were its only guests. It wasn't cheap at 150RMB, or thirty bucks. But to us it seemed like an oasis. It wasn't even noon when we checked in, but we were thankful to put an early end to our day. We spent the rest of the day in bed recovering from the previous two nights and catching up on our journals. We also washed our clothes and tried to dry them on the room's radiators. The radiators were so hot we had to keep moving our clothes around to keep them from getting singed. Still, we were happy to have dry clothes to wear again—singed or not. The only time we left our room was for lunch and dinner in the hotel restaurant, where we were the only customers. By the time we went to sleep that night we agreed it was a perfect day and we hoped for more just like it.

The next morning was unexpected. We woke to a glorious blue sky and as much sunlight as our eyes could stand. When we went outside for a stroll, we had to squint. We looked for some shade and thankfully found it along a path that led through a pine forest. The path ended a few minutes later at the Lushan Museum. We arrived just as someone inside unlocked the door. We were just taking a stroll, but we couldn't turn

Waterfall on Lushan

down the chance to see what was inside. Of course, there were exhibits of the mountain's plants and animals and insects, but more interesting was the exhibit of Chairman Mao's bedroom and office as they looked during the famous Lushan Plenary, the one held in 1959 when P'eng Te-huai criticized the Great Helmsman for his Great Leap Backward. Two decades earlier, Chiang Kai-shek also frequented the mountain. There wasn't a road then, and he had to be carried up in a sedan chair. The museum recreated his bedroom, including his Western-style toilet customized so that he could squat with his shoes on the rim.

In the end, the world outside was more interesting. We returned to the hotel and collected our bags, and asked the desk clerk how to get down the mountain. Unfortunately, the Lulin was located on the south end of the summit, far from public transport, and we didn't feel like hiking to the north end with our bags. We decided to throw money at the problem and asked the desk clerk to arrange for a car to take us down the mountain. Five minutes later, a driver pulled up, and we headed downhill. It was an expensive indulgence, at 200RMB, but considering our lethargy, we agreed it was the right choice.

On our way up the mountain, we were still half-asleep and didn't pay attention to the road. There were curves, but they actually helped rock us back to sleep. Going down was a different story, and we didn't sleep. The driver said there were four hundred curves, and he might have been right. We didn't count. We were more concerned with our survival. But we did survive, and in less than thirty minutes we were at the Chiuchiang bus station and grateful to be there.

Chiuchiang probably has its charms, but we didn't stay long enough to find out what they were. After stashing our bags in the bus station's luggage depository, we caught the next bus to Hukou. It was only thirty kilometers to the northeast and was the scene of a natural phenomenon we had heard about and wanted to see for ourselves. As it turned out, the bus ride was even stranger. By the time we got off an hour later, half the people on the bus had some of our money—and not from picking our pockets.

When foreigners came to China in those days, they weren't allowed to get RMB, or local currency, from banks. They had to change their dollars or pounds or francs for Foreign Exchange Certificates, better known as FEC, which were supposed to have the same value as RMB. Several years earlier, when I changed my dollars for RMB on the black market, I received anywhere from 20 percent to 40 percent more than the official FEC rate. By 1991, I was lucky if I could get 10 percent more, and I was often glad to trade one-to-one just to have a supply of RMB. So when someone on the bus asked to change money, we agreed. We even agreed to change even-steven: one FEC for one RMB.

This was a busload of farmers going back to their villages, and when one of them heard we were exchanging FEC, he whispered to the others that the official rate was five to one, not one to one. Obviously, he was confusing FEC with dollars. We tried to explain, but it was no use. The stampede was on. Everyone on the bus, including the driver and the conductress, got out their wads of bills and lined up. We could hardly object. In the areas where we had been traveling, storekeepers often had never seen FEC and refused to accept anything but RMB. By the time we ran out of FEC, we had enough RMB to last the rest of the trip. Meanwhile, our fellow passengers chuckled at the thought of making a five-to-one profit off a couple of hillbilly foreigners. It was a good-natured group that dropped us off in Hukou and drove away with our money.

The reason we made the effort to come to Hukou was to see the Yangtze again. Of course, we could have done that in Chiuchiang, where we got off the boat the previous night. But as the Yangtze flowed past Hukou, it changed color. That was something we wanted to see. In Chinese, the name *Hukou* means "lake mouth." In this case, it was at the mouth of one of the largest freshwater lakes in China, namely Poyanghu. Hukou was where the lake emptied into the Yangtze, and the place where people could observe what took place when their waters met was Stone Bell Hill.

From where the bus let us off, it was a ten-minute walk through the edge of a village to the park that enclosed the hill's pleasure gardens and pavilions where many of China's most famous poets stopped to drain their cups. Ironically, the painting Steve bought in Hsiangtan from the curator of the future Ch'i Pai-shih Museum portrayed the poet Su Tung-p'o standing in his boat beneath Stone Bell Hill nine hundred years ago drinking a toast to the moon. After paying the admission fee of 10RMB, we followed a path of stone steps to the promontory where we had a clear view of the place below which Su stood in his little boat. It was, as we had expected, a remarkable sight: instead of mixing, the blue-green water of Poyang Lake flowed alongside the red-brown water of the Yangtze without mixing. The brochure we bought at the park entrance said they flowed like that for three kilometers before they merged.

It was, indeed, a curious phenomenon. But once we had seen it, we didn't linger. It was eleven o'clock, and we wanted to get back to Chiuchiang and Lushan. We walked back to the highway and waited for the next bus. The village below Stone Bell Hill was a farming village, and the crowd that gathered around us soon numbered in the hundreds. When this happened earlier at Huaminglou, we narrowly escaped the clutches of the local police. This time the crowd worked to our advantage. Express buses weren't scheduled to stop there. But when one came along, it had no choice. Once more we waved good-bye to two hundred new friends.

An hour later, we were back in Chiuchiang. We had already toured the city's most famous sight, namely, Lushan, albeit in the fog. But there was more to Lushan than its summit, and we wanted to tour its foothills as well. Unfortunately, there wasn't any public transportation to the places we wanted to visit. So after collecting our bags, we walked outside the bus station and flagged down a taxi. After a brief negotiation, we settled on 150RMB, or thirty bucks, for a half-day circumambulation. It was already one o'clock when we finally set off. We weren't sure where we were going to spend the night. But it didn't matter. We were traveling, and traveling in comfort for a change.

From Chiuchiang, we followed the highway that skirted the mountain's eastern flank for about twenty kilometers then turned onto a side road and drove into a forest. A few minutes later, the road ended at another of the four great centers of Confucian learning in China. We had already visited one of the four on Yuehlushan near Changsha. This one was called Pailutung Shuyuan, or White Deer Cave Academy.

White Deer Cave Academy's white deer

The name came from a deer that often visited the man who first opened a school here in the eighth century. Unlike the academy outside Changsha, White Deer Cave Academy was set in a secluded forest beside a babbling stream. It was a beautiful setting. But its setting wasn't the reason for its reputation. Its fame came from its long history as a preeminent center of learning. Although it had been a school as early as the eighth century, it wasn't until the twelfth century that it became one of the Big Four. This was due to Chu Hsi (1130–1200), who also helped establish the academy on Yuehlushan.

Besides being governor of the province, Chu Hsi was also one of China's most famous philosophers and commentators on the Confucian classics. Even though his commentaries were written over eight hundred years ago, no Chinese today would think of studying or discussing the Confucian canon without first seeing what Chu Hsi had to say. While he was governor, he often came here to write and to lecture. He also convinced the emperor to favor the academy with imperial patronage, and it remained a center of higher education until modern times.

As we walked through the front gate and toured its halls, everywhere hung the calligraphy of the notable teachers who had taught here, including the neo-Confucian, Wang Yang-ming (1472–1529). Like the Confucian academy on Yuehlushan, it was no longer an academy but a museum to the past. But it was still worth visiting. It was peaceful and cool in the dappled sunlight that fell through its thousand-year-old trees. And there was even a small restaurant and a dozen or so rooms for people who wanted to spend the night. If we had known that earlier, that's what we would have done. But we had already hired our car and driver, and we had more places to see. After pausing to pay our respects before the stone statue of the white deer, we returned to our car.

Back on the main road, we continued south five kilometers and turned off again and drove through another forest to the foot of one of Lushan's more famous peaks. It's called Hsiufeng, or Flowering Peak, and it's been attracting visitors for more than a thousand years. There were vendors selling food, and we suddenly realized we had missed lunch and sat down near the trailhead long enough to have a bowl of dumplings.

Then we started up the stone steps that led to the peak. We weren't planning to hike all the way to the top. We just wanted to get a taste of the mountain. Fortunately, it wasn't the weekend, and we had the trail to ourselves—or almost to ourselves. Shadowing our every step were half a dozen sedan-chair porters trying to convince us that the only proper way to climb the peak was in a chair. It may have been the way Chiang Kai-shek climbed the mountain, but we weren't Chiang Kai-shek.

As we continued on, the price dropped from 50RMB, to 40, to 30, to 25 and finally 20. Still, we preferred to walk. Along the way, we passed a stele inscribed with the image of Kuan-yin, the Bodhisattva of Compassion. It was carved 300 years ago and was all that was left of a famous Buddhist temple that once occupied the spot. We followed the trail further and eventually came to Dragon Pool. Just beyond the pool's black waters, we sat down at a pavilion that offered a wonderful view of Hsiufeng. It looked like the perfect place to end our hike. It was a beautiful setting, but we didn't give it the time it deserved. The afternoon was half gone, and we had miles to go. As soon as we caught our breaths, we headed back down and returned to the main road again.

Once more, we headed south. Ten minutes later, we began stopping every kilometer or so to ask farmers the location of the hot spring sanatorium. We weren't interested in the sanatorium itself but in the village next to it. The third farmer we asked said we had gone a bit too far. We backtracked and parked at the side of the highway. About two hundred meters from the road was a grove of ancient trees next to a group of mud-brick houses surrounded by rice fields and mulberry orchards. This was the place we were looking for. From the highway, we zigzagged our way across the rice fields to the place where the poet T'ao Yuan-ming (365–427) built his hut in the early years of the fifth century.

T'ao Yuan-ming has always been one of my favorite poets, and I'm not alone. Most Chinese rank him among their greatest literary figures. He served as an official for a brief period, but, as he put it, "How could I lower myself, for a few sacks of rice." At the age of forty, he retired and spent the remaining twenty-two years of his life in the shadow of Lushan writing poems and tending a garden and getting drunk with his

Dragon Pool and Hsiufeng Peak

neighbors. One of his most famous poems is the fifth of a twenty-poem series entitled "Drinking Poems":

I built my hut in the world of men
but I hear no noise of cart or horse
you ask how can this be
when the mind travels so does the place
picking chrysanthemums along the eastern fence
I lose myself in the southern hills
the mountain air the sunset light
birds returning home together
in this there is a truth
I'd explain but I've forgotten the words

T'ao Yuan-ming also wrote stories, one of which everyone in China knows—even foreigners. It's called "Peach Blossom Spring." It seems that one day a fisherman noticed peach blossoms floating down a stream not far from where we were standing. He was curious and wondered where the peach blossoms were coming from. He had never seen peach trees in that area before and decided to find the source of the petals. He walked along the shore and followed the stream until he came to a place where the water flowed out of a crevice in the rocks. With some difficulty, he managed to squeeze through the crevice. Suddenly, he came out into a beautiful valley. There were people living in the valley, but they wore old-fashioned clothes. And when he spoke to them, they answered in a dialect he barely understood. They welcomed him into their homes and told him their ancestors had discovered the valley several hundred years earlier while trying to escape the oppression of the Ch'in dynasty. No one had left the valley since then, and they were curious about the course of the intervening centuries. Once the fisherman had answered their questions, he said he had to return home. The people escorted him back to the crevice, but before saying good-bye, they asked him not to reveal the whereabouts of their valley.

The fisherman agreed, but on his way back to his village, he marked his route so he could remember how to get back. And the first thing he

View of mountains south of T'ao Yuan-ming's old home

did after he returned home was to tell the local magistrate about his discovery. The official sent his assistants to accompany the fisherman to find the hidden valley, but they never found it again. And the location of Peach Blossom Spring remains a mystery to this day.

While we were standing there in the little village where this story was written, several of the author's descendants came out to see what we were doing. The place wasn't on the tourist map, and the villagers had never seen a foreigner before. But they were friendly and even showed us the spot where the poet's farmhouse once stood. The spot they pointed to was beside a small stream and next to the group of trees we had seen from the highway. The trees were ancient and must have been hundreds of years old. There was also a marker that had been put there by some government agency announcing that this was, indeed, the site of T'ao Yuan-ming's old home. Beyond the small grove of trees and mud huts, rice fields and mulberry orchards stretched in all directions. The huge green shadow of Lushan rose on the western horizon, and one of its spurs rose to the south—the "southern hills" T'ao Yuan-ming gazed at

House of T'ao Yuan-ming's last lineal descendent

in the fifth of his "Drinking Poems." Again, we had to tear ourselves away. However, before leaving I asked his descendants about the location of their ancestor's grave. They confirmed the directions I had written down from another traveler's account, and we returned to our car.

A few kilometers later, we came to a crossroads at the village of Aikou. We turned north and began driving along Lushan's western flank back toward Chiuchiang. Two kilometers later, we turned off the paved road onto a dirt road that led toward the mountain. A sign in Chinese said NO ADMITTANCE. We told our driver to ignore it, and we continued up the road. A few minutes later, we came to the entrance of a military base. The guards were surprised. So were we. No one mentioned a military base. We got out and walked over to the gate, and said we wanted to visit T'ao Yuan-ming's grave. The guards said no one was allowed on the base. There really wasn't much we could say, but we asked if we could talk to their commanding officer. Maybe, we thought, they could make an exception for some poetry pilgrims.

The guards called someone on the phone, and a few minutes later, two officers drove up in a jeep. The military base was used by the navy for munitions storage and for special forces training. We could tell by the sound of gunfire that some sort of weapons exercise was in progress. When the officers came over to talk with us, they repeated what the guards had already told us. It was useless. No one, they said, was allowed on the base without permission. And clearly we didn't have permission. We had no choice but to pay our respects from the main gate, which we did by pouring some whiskey into three cups, offering it to the sky gods, then drinking it ourselves. Then we returned to the highway and continued our northward journey along Lushan's western flank.

The road we were on led back to Chiuchiang, but halfway there we turned off one last time. Our final stop of the day was Tunglin Temple. It was one of the most famous Buddhist temples in China. Most Chinese Buddhists practice Pure Land Buddhism, and this was where the teachings of that school were first put into practice. The monk who started it all was Hui-yuan (334–416). While he was living here, he came into possession of some newly-translated Buddhist sutras that encouraged devotees to seek rebirth in the Pure Land of Amita Buddha, the Buddha of the Infinite, where enlightenment was said to be much easier than in this land of endless distraction. Hui-yuan gathered a group of disciples and in 402 AD founded the White Lotus Society, whose members vowed to seek rebirth in the Pure Land by chanting Amita Buddha's name, which they pronounced "*Omitofo.*"

The temple was still here, but it looked like we had arrived too late. Most temples closed their gates around five o'clock, if not before, and it was nearly six. From the dirt parking lot, we walked across a stone bridge that spanned a small stream and approached the temple's main gate. The gate was closed, but we yelled "*Namo Omitofo*"—"Homage to the Buddha of the Infinite" and waited. We yelled several times, but no one answered. Finally, just as we were about to turn away, the gate slowly creaked opened. The monk who opened it said, "*Omitofo*" in reply. Before we had a chance to ask if the temple was still open, he smiled and asked us if we wanted to spend the night. Naturally, we accepted.

We walked back to the taxi and collected our bags, paid the driver, and walked back across the bridge and through the temple gate again.

Every temple has a guest hall where visitors who want to spend the night register. The monk at the gate led us inside, and we signed our names, and the guest manager led us to a room upstairs. The monks had already had their dinner, but we had some peanuts and crackers in our bags, and that was enough. After taking cold showers, we lay down for the night and fell asleep listening to the monks ring the temple bell 108 times, once for every form of liberation from all the myriad forms of suffering, including hangovers.

淨土 禪

8. Pure Land & Zen

Our sweet dreams to the contrary, we didn't wake up in the Pure Land. It was the same old world of red dust. But at least it was temple dust. It was so quiet. Breakfast was at six, and someone knocked on our door, but we slept on. We were on vacation. Finally, about eight o'clock we packed up our stuff and walked outside, and went to thank

Tunglin Monastery front gate and Tiger Stream Bridge

the guest manager for letting us spend the night. When we entered the guest hall, the guest manager was talking to a much older monk. The older monk turned out to be the abbot, Master Kuo-yi. We thanked them both for their hospitality and told them we wanted to pay our respects to Hui-yuan before leaving. It was Hui-yuan who initiated the practice of Pure Land Buddhism in China. Since then it had become the major form of Buddhism in the Middle Kingdom.

The abbot led us to the shrine hall where Hui-yuan led the first group of devotees in the practice of chanting the name of Amita Buddha in order to be reborn in the Pure Land. Despite Tunglin's fame as a center of Buddhist practice, it had only been returned to the monks twelve years earlier, following the government's reestablishment of religious freedom in 1979. Since then Kuo-yi had convinced the local government to return a thousand acres of agricultural and forest land to the monastery in addition to the land on which the buildings stood. He also helped raise money to rebuild the shrine halls and monks' quarters. The hall where Hui-yuan conducted the first Pure Land ceremonies had also been rebuilt, and we went inside and lit some incense. Afterwards, the abbot told us that Hui-yuan's remains were in a much smaller shrine hall on the dirt path that led back to the main road. Since we wanted to return to the main road anyway, we grabbed our bags and followed his directions. Two minutes later, we were there.

Sitting outside in the morning sun was an old monk. He was fingering a long string of beads. But as soon as he saw us, he got up and waved for us to enter the shrine hall. We left our bags by the doorway and walked inside. As we did, he handed each of us three sticks of incense, which we lit and placed in the incense burner in front of Hui-yuan's statue. While we were watching our sticks of incense burn, the monk insisted we sit down and join him for a cup of tea. He said in the old days the trail to the summit of Lushan began in front of Tunglin Temple. It took three and a half hours, he said, to walk from the temple to the top of the mountain, and hundreds of people stopped at Hui-yuan's shrine every day to pay their respects. Now that there was a road to the top, days went by between visitors. He was glad to have someone to talk to.

He could have done better than us; we were anxious to move on. We had a long way to go and weren't sure how we were going to get there. After chatting for as long as we dared, we thanked him for the tea and continued along the path that led to the road. Halfway there, the path also led past Hsilin, or West Grove Temple. It was a Buddhist nunnery, and next to it was a forty-meter-high pagoda. The pagoda was very impressive, and we walked over to get a closer look. There was a high wall around the base, and the gate was locked. But while we were looking for a way in, we met a nun working in the nunnery's vegetable garden. She stopped working long enough to tell us the reason for the wall. She said during the Cultural Revolution, a group of Red Guards broke into the temple and started destroying everything in sight. One of them climbed the pagoda and started smashing the carved reliefs on the outside. She said she tried to stop him, but he wouldn't listen. He lost his footing and fell to his death. Ever since then, there has been a wall around the pagoda to keep people away.

She, too, invited us to join her for tea, but we were in our travel mode. We thanked her and returned to the path. A minute later, we were standing at the edge of the paved road that brought us there the previous day. We put our bags down and waited for a bus heading south. Normally it didn't take more than a few minutes to flag down a bus. There was always something heading our way. But not this time. After waiting for over an hour, it finally dawned on us that we had arrived by taxi and that buses were probably using a different road. Since it was too far to walk with our packs to the nearest road where there were buses, we started waving at trucks. We stood there waving for another hour before a driver finally stopped and gave us a ride. We threw our bags in the back and squeezed into the cab. Like truck drivers the world over, he stopped because he was bored. And like truck drivers the world over, he thought the people running his country were idiots and was glad to have someone willing to listen to his complaints. Even though we didn't understand most of what he said, we nodded our heads often enough. He was happy, and so were we.

Two hours later, he dropped us off in the town of Te-an. It was already

Hsilin Nunnery pagoda

one o'clock, and the next bus heading south wasn't scheduled to leave until two. At least we had time for noodles. The reason for our slow progress was due to the location of our destination. It wasn't on a main road. But there was a bus that went nearby, and we were on it at two o'clock. But it didn't leave at two o'clock. It sat there in the bus station parking lot for thirty minutes while the driver dealt with some personal matter. Even when it did leave, it didn't travel for more than a minute without stopping to pick someone up or to let someone off. Three hours later, we finally got off at a wide place in the road called Chiuchin, or Dragon Crossing. It was the sort of place truck drivers stopped. The reason we got off there was because it was near our destination. But the sun was on its way down, and it was too late to try to find transportation. There weren't any hotels either, just one building posing as a restaurant that had a room upstairs with four beds. So at least we had a place to sleep and a place to eat, not that we ate that well or slept that well. It was a port in a storm.

After eating some very dismal fried rice and drinking a few warm beers, we went up to our room. As we were settling down for the night, the landlady came up with a thermos of hot water, and we asked her where the toilet was. She led us outside the door to the balcony and pointed to the pond below. Before retiring for the night, we blinded a couple of fish. What else could we do? At least it was cheap: dinner, beer, and lodging for three tired travelers was 32RMB, or less than $6.

The next morning, we woke to the sound of truck horns and walked out to the road to arrange transportation to the place we wanted to visit. Initial negotiations proved useless. The drivers of the tractors and motorcycles with carryalls wanted at least 120RMB to take us there. It was only twenty kilometers, and I was hoping to pay half that much. I had discovered that in such situations the best policy was to quote a reasonable price, then walk away. Sure enough, one of the drivers came running after us. He agreed to take us there for 50RMB.

We climbed aboard the carryall welded to his motorcycle and left Dragon Crossing in the dust. After about five kilometers, we turned onto a dirt road that led to the top of Yunchushan, or Cloud Rest Mountain.

That was our destination. Yunchushan was the final resting place of Hsu-yun, or Empty Cloud, China's most famous Zen monk of the past century. He spent his last years on the mountain and died there in 1959 at the age of 120. How could we not pay our respects?

Once we began zigzagging our way up the dirt road that led to the top, it soon became apparent why our driver had agreed to take us for 50RMB, while his colleagues wanted twice that. Whenever the slope exceeded ten degrees, we had to get out and walk. It took nearly two hours to go the last ten kilometers.

Just before the end of the road, we passed a building that claimed to be a hotel. It turned out to be closed, and we wondered what a hotel was doing up here anyway. We continued on, and a minute later arrived at the front gate of Chenju Temple. It was like nothing we had seen before. The world of red dust clearly ended at the gate. Beyond was a valley of rice fields and lotus ponds and a large temple at the end of the valley surrounded on three sides by the forested slopes of Cloud Rest Mountain. A more perfect setting for a Zen monastery would be hard to imagine. We found out later that the temple had only recently regained control of all the land inside the gate, which consisted of more than a thousand acres.

We got out of the carryall and paid the driver. Obviously, he wouldn't be needing our help going downhill. Before walking through the gate, we went over to the memorial hall that housed Empty Cloud's remains. It was a hundred meters to the left, and the archway was inscribed with Empty Cloud's nickname: Huanyou Laojen, The Old Illusory Traveler.

After paying our respects, we returned to the front gate and followed a path of stone steps along the edge of two large ponds. Empty Cloud helped dredge one of them during his last spring. The year was 1959, and he was approaching his 120th birthday. When one of his disciples suggested celebrating the occasion, he said:

> *I'm like a candle in the wind. I've achieved nothing. When
> I think of this, I'm ashamed of my hollow reputation. My
> hundred years in this world of trouble has been like a dream,
> like an illusion, and not worthy of such concern. Since birth*

Mausoleum containing Empty Cloud's remains

leads to death, a wise person should set their mind on the Way instead. How can I indulge in the worldly custom of celebrating a birthday? I appreciate your thoughtfulness, but I ask that you stop this plan of celebrating mine in order not to add to my sins.

He died two months later.

We followed the path past the ponds and the rice fields to the monastery where he spent his last years. Empty Cloud was credited with reviving the practice of Zen in China, and he is easily the country's most famous monk of the past few centuries. We had come to pay our respects, but we also wanted to meet another monk we had heard about, a monk people called Ch'i-fo, the Eccentric Buddha. We had heard he was living on Yunchushan.

After we reached the temple, we made our way to the guest hall. As at Tunglin Temple, this was where visitors came who wanted to spend the night. The previous night at Tunglin Temple the guest manager whisked us through the registration process, but this time the monk in charge of receiving guests said we couldn't stay without a letter of introduction or some proof that we were actually followers of the Way. Our saying so, he said, did not constitute proof. We were at a loss. Finally, we got out our prayer beads, the ones monks and nuns use to count their recitations. But this, too, proved insufficient. The monk said anyone could buy prayer beads. Since there wasn't anything else we could say or do to prove that we followed the path of the Buddha (although in his dust), we had no choice but to turn and head for the door. But before we reached the door, I stopped and turned around.

I told the monk that I had proof, and I rolled up my left sleeve. The scars had faded a bit, but they were still visible: three circles where three cones of incense had burned down fifteen years earlier. I had been living in a Zen monastery in Taiwan for several years, and the abbot decided it was time I had a souvenir of my stay. It was part of a Buddhist initiation ceremony. Monks and nuns burn incense cones on their shaved heads. Lay disciples burn them on their forearms. The actual burning

*Chenju Monastery Abbot, Master Yi-ch'eng with author at Empty Cloud
Memorial Hall (photo by Steven R. Johnson)*

lasts about ten minutes, and, of course, it's painful. But it's what Chinese Buddhists do, and I wanted to make the abbot happy. I showed the guest manager my scars, and he showed us to a room.

After we dropped our bags in our room, the guest manager led us to the abbot's quarters. The abbot's name was Yi-ch'eng. When we entered his reception room, we wondered whether or not to ask him about the Eccentric Buddha, who was reportedly somewhere on the mountain. But he didn't give us a chance. While his attendant poured us cups of tea, he told us the history of the temple. Then he took us on a tour. Normally abbots were too busy to guide people around their monasteries, but it turned out Yi-ch'eng was not your normal abbot.

He began with the new memorial hall built next to the cowshed where Empty Cloud spent his last years. When the great Zen master came here in the winter of 1953, he was 114, and the place was in ruins. The only structure with a roof was a cowshed, so that was where he lived. But because of his reputation, Empty Cloud was soon joined by several hundred other monks, and within three years they managed to reconstruct many of the monastery's buildings. Empty Cloud, though, continued to live in the cowshed until his death in 1959.

In the center of the memorial hall next to his former residence there was a bronze statue of the old Zen master. It had white eyebrows and a white beard that made it look alive. There was also a display case that contained some of Hsu-yun's personal items, including his patched robe and his cloth shoes. When I thought about the fine robes and comfortable accommodations of other monks we had met in China, we felt embarrassed. Their dedication to the path of the Buddha seemed so superficial compared with that of a monk like Hsu-lao, or Old Empty, as he was called by those who knew him.

After we paid our respects, Yi-ch'eng led us to the temple's unfinished meditation hall in the monastery's south wing. It was being built entirely out of wood without any nails—all mortise and tenon construction. Even if it had been made of cement, we still would have been impressed. Nearly all the Buddhist temples we had seen in China were devoted to Pure Land practice, which revolved around chanting the name of

Amita Buddha. And such practice usually took place in a shrine hall. A meditation hall in a Pure Land temple wouldn't make sense. But Chenju Temple was a Zen temple, and the heart of Zen practice is meditation. Hence, a meditation hall is the most important structure in a Zen monastery, and Chenju Temple's new one was impressive.

The new hall, though, wasn't finished, and we asked Yi-ch'eng where the monks meditated while it was under construction. He smiled and led us to the monastery's north wing. At the end of a long corridor, he lifted a heavy blanket that covered a doorway and waved for us to follow him inside. Once our eyes got used to the darkness, we realized he had led us into the old meditation hall. Sitting on cushions on a wooden platform that lined the hall's four walls were more than a hundred monks.

Yi-ch'eng then began circling the room and motioned for us to follow. It must have been a strange sight: the abbot of the monastery followed by three bearded foreigners wearing sunglasses. As we walked past the monks, trances cracked and eyes bulged. When Yi-ch'eng finally led us back outside, he couldn't keep from laughing, and neither could we. Suddenly we realized we didn't need to ask the identity of the Eccentric Buddha. We had not only met him, we had seen him in action.

After showing us the new memorial hall and scaring the monks in the old meditation hall, Yi-ch'eng led us outside past the monastery's front steps and along a trail that skirted the far side of the two ponds. The trail ended at the temple's cemetery. There were a dozen small stupas, and Yi-ch'eng pointed out the one that belonged to the monk who founded the monastery. His name was Tao-jung. He came here in the T'ang dynasty, 1,200 years ago. In the centuries since then, the temple had become a major center of Zen practice in China, with as many as 1,500 monks in residence. And it remained a major Zen center until the Japanese destroyed it during the Second World War.

Below Tao-jung's grave and next to the stream that fed the ponds, Yi-ch'eng pointed to a boulder. He said the poet Su Tung-p'o often sat here with the temple's abbot 900 years ago discussing Zen. Having shown us all he had time for, Yi-ch'eng returned to the temple. Instead of following him back to the monastery, we sat down and spent the

Chenju Monastery and rice fields

afternoon listening to the song of the grasshoppers. Steve took out some marijuana he brought with him. It seemed like the perfect place and the perfect time to smoke a reefer. And that was what we did. It was, of course, a beautiful day.

Just before sunset, our reverie was interrupted when three girls suddenly came down the trail from a nearby peak. They stopped and asked us what we were doing here. We told them we were paying our respects to the previous abbots of the temple. Then we asked what they were doing there. They said they were coming back from a hike. They said they grew up at the monastery during the Cultural Revolution, when the monks were driven out and the place was turned into a farm commune. They said they were just visiting, and if we wanted dinner, we'd better follow them, which was what we did. Back at the old commune, we enjoyed a simple vegetarian meal in the dining hall reserved for guests. Then we retired for the night. But we didn't go to sleep. While we were lying in bed writing in our journals by candlelight—our room didn't have any electricity—there was a knock on the door. A young monk

Chenju Monastery at dawn

entered and introduced himself and spent the next two hours telling us everything we ever wanted to know about Heidegger and Wittgenstein. Hearing about modern European philosophy in an ancient Chinese Zen monastery was as strange as meeting the Eccentric Buddha. All in all, it was a perfect day.

Once again, we slept past breakfast. It was getting to be a habit. I'm not sure we needed the extra sleep. We didn't stay up that late. But it was our way of reminding ourselves that we were blessed by such good fortune, why not enjoy it? Our only worry was how we were going to get down the mountain. But it wasn't really a worry. The road was downhill, and our feet worked fine.

After we finally got up, we went to say good-bye to Yi-ch'eng and to thank him for letting us spend the night. The previous day, when he took us to the temple graveyard, he also pointed out the grave of another monk who had helped him understand Zen when he was still a young monk. The monk's name was Hsing-fu. He served as the abbot of Chenju Temple after Empty Cloud died. After Hsing-fu died, Yi-ch'eng became abbot. Since then, Yi-ch'eng had picked up the nickname of Ch'i-fo, or Eccentric Buddha, because he used every trick in the Buddhist canon to enlighten his disciples. We had heard of him for years and expected someone wilder and crazier. He turned out to be as sweet as our grandmothers.

He told us if we stayed another day, we could take the monastery bus down the mountain. He said the bus brought pilgrims to the mountain once or twice a week from the provincial capital of Nanchang. Nanchang was where we were headed ourselves, but we decided not to wait for the bus. After we said good-bye to Yi-ch'eng, the guest manager picked up Steve's pack. It was full of camera gear and was the heaviest of our three packs. Then he led us out of the monastery and down the dirt road that led up the mountain. We had no choice but to follow him.

While we were walking, we walked past the "hotel" we had seen on the way up and asked the guest manager about it. He said the monastery used it whenever they had a big ceremony. He said that the week before we arrived, they held a ceremony that 1,600 people attended. He said not everyone spent the night there, but several hundred of them did. Even though our room at the monastery didn't have electricity, we were glad we didn't stay at the hotel. It looked bleak.

After walking about two kilometers, the guest manager finally stopped and took off Steve's pack. He was dripping with sweat, but he had made his point. He was taking us as far as he could. He pointed to a stone path that led off to the side and down through a forest. He said it was the old trail, and it would save us a couple of hours. We bowed in thanks then headed down.

He was right. If we had walked down the road, it would have taken us at least three hours, but the trail only took an hour. As it finally flattened out at the foot of the mountain, the trail led past a small temple. It was a nunnery, and the abbess saw us coming. She waved for us to follow her inside, and she insisted we stay for lunch. We had missed breakfast and were glad to oblige. It was only ten o'clock, but she and her fellow nuns made us an early lunch of freshly cut bamboo shoots and homemade tofu. Once again, the road gods were smiling on us.

After we ate as much as we dared, we said good-bye then followed the road that ran past the nunnery and past the provincial agricultural college out to the highway. Less than a minute after reaching the highway, we were on a bus bound for Nanchang. But it was not like any of the buses we had been on before. Instead of hard benches, it had individual seats. We had never before experienced such luxury on a bus in China.

For the next two hours, we drove through a landscape of hills terraced with rice and tea. It wasn't at all boring, but it would have been a lot less interesting if the driver hadn't stopped to pick up an old lady and her child. Apparently, the old lady had never been on such a high-class bus before either. When she heard how much a ticket cost, she spent the next hour arguing with the conductress about the price. Our vocabularies were increased immeasurably by the epithets that she had probably spent years perfecting. Finally, she ran out of steam and paid the price, and finally we arrived in Nanchang. We got off in the center of town and walked to the nearest hotel. The first one was the five-star Kiangsi Guesthouse, where they wanted 280RMB for a triple. Next door, the three-star Kiangsi Hotel wanted seventy-five, and they didn't ask to see the scars on our arms.

南昌

9. Nanchang

Waking up at the Kiangsi Hotel was not the same as waking up at Chenju Temple. Instead of mountains and rice fields and lotus ponds and the stillness of a monastery, we woke up surrounded by the cement and noise of another urban explosion. We were in Nanchang, the capital of Kiangsi. It was our fourth provincial capital: Kuangchou, Changsha, Wuhan, and now Nanchang.

Painting and poem carved on stone

Our hotel was on August First Road a block or two from August First Square. August First was the date in 1927 when the Communists launched their armed struggle against the Nationalist government. The previous year, Chiang Kai-shek began his Northern Expedition to wrest control of the country from local warlords. He was given charge of all revolutionary forces, including those controlled by the Communists. When he reached Shanghai the following spring, he decided to eliminate any future contenders for power and massacred thousands of Communists and their supporters. Chou En-lai and other leftist leaders managed to escape and regroup in Nanchang. And on August 1ˢᵗ, they launched their counteroffensive. It took them twenty-two years, but they finally succeeded in giving Chiang and the Nationalists the boot in 1949 and formed the People's Republic of China.

Right across the street from our hotel was the Memorial Hall to the Martyrs of the Revolution. After breakfast, we poked our heads inside, but we weren't familiar with the names, and there weren't any explanations in English. It was a period we knew almost nothing about. Our ignorance was in part due to our anti-Communist upbringing. America had its own Cultural Revolution. It was called the McCarthy Era, when people who were suspected of having leftist sympathies were fired from their jobs and even put in prison. I can still remember the maps in school with China and Russia colored red, and our teachers telling us that Communism was taking over the world and that this was something bad. In fact, that's still what they say about Communism. Private wealth good. Sharing bad. So naturally, we never learned about what was going on in China.

A few blocks away, we also visited the Nanchang Uprising Memorial Hall. It was located in the same building used by the rebels for their headquarters. They didn't use it long. They were driven out of Nanchang by Nationalist forces three days later. Once again, all the displays and explanations were in Chinese about a period of history we knew nothing about. It just as well could have been about the Middle Ages. We continued walking down the same street until it ended at the banks of the Kan River.

Nanchang's August First Monument

Rising a few blocks to the north was the towering structure of the Tengwangke, the third of ancient China's three famous towers. We had already seen the other two. This one was first built in 653, more than four hundred years after the other two. It was built by the Prince of T'eng—hence its name: the Tower of Prince T'eng. It had been destroyed and rebuilt many times and had spent the last hundred years in ruins until 1989, when it once more rose from the rubble. Like Yellow Crane Tower in Wuhan, it too was rebuilt out of cement, which was just as well. It would have taken a whole forest to recreate this fifty-seven-meter-high monument to ostentation.

As we looked at the tower, we thought about whether we wanted to climb its stairs. We had already climbed Wuhan's Yellow Crane Tower for a view of that city's smokestacks. We decided one forgettable urban panorama was enough. Obviously, we weren't really tourists. We walked past the tower and a few blocks later stopped to inquire at the Harbor Terminal about the possibility of leaving Nanchang by boat.

Just as the Hsiang River defines the landscape of Hunan, the Kan River defines Kiangsi. After its wide waters pass Nanchang, they empty into Poyang Lake then into the Yangtze. We had already visited the spot where the two waters met but didn't merge. There was another river that emptied into Poyang Lake, and there was a boat that left Nanchang and traveled up the other river to our next destination, which was China's porcelain capital of Chingtechen. We scanned the list of departures listed above the ticket window. Sure enough, there was a boat scheduled to leave the next day. For centuries, the bulk of Chingtechen's porcelain had been transported by boat via Poyang Lake into the Yangtze then to the rest of China. This was true of all ancient porcelain centers in China. Rivers were smooth. Roads were not. Unfortunately, Kiangsi turned out to be in the midst of a three-year drought, and it was late fall. The woman selling tickets told us to come back next summer, and to pray for rain.

Since a boat was out of the question, we flagged down a taxi and went to the train station and bought tickets for the eleven o'clock night train to Chingtechen. That left us with the rest of the day and only one place we wanted to visit. Kiangsi had never numbered among China's wealthier provinces, but its native sons included many of the country's leading artists, writers, and intellectuals. The man we were interested in was Chu Ta (1626–1705), better known by his sobriquet: Pa-ta Shan-jen. He was born in Nanchang into a distant line of the imperial family. He was a descendant of Chu Ch'uan, the Prince of Ning, who entertained delusions that he was the rightful heir to the Ming throne and died for acting on such delusions.

When Chu Ta was in his twenties, China was overrun by the Manchus, and Nanchang was starved into submission. The Ming dynasty came to an end, and the Ch'ing dynasty began. Chu Ta, however, refused to serve the new rulers and became a Buddhist monk. But instead of meditating or chanting scriptures, he devoted himself to painting, calligraphy, and seal carving. His monk's robe was just a cover. Instead of giving up his wealth, he used it to build a retreat in Nanchang's southern suburbs on a site occupied by Taoist temples for more than 2,000 years. To Taoists it was known as Tienningkuan, or Tienning Observatory, after their interest in observing the movements of celestial phenomena as having a possible bearing on movements within the body. Chu Ta changed the name to Chingyunpu, or Blue Cloud Garden.

From the train station, it was a ten-kilometer bus ride. It was a slow ride, but we had nothing but time. We got off on Chingyunpu Road, and there it was. It was easy to spot, with its long white walls completely surrounded by ponds. It looked like an island. In fact, it was an island. As we walked across the bridge and through the front gate, we couldn't help wonder how a place of such delicate beauty had survived in a city of such unrelieved ugliness.

Since Pa-ta Shan-jen lived here, his former residence had become a memorial hall. The hall, which was actually a series of wings and courtyards and corridors, was located at the rear of the grounds. It looked like similar memorial halls we had seen. But what surprised us was that it had several dozen of his paintings—originals according to the caretakers, unlike the Ch'i Pai-shih Memorial Hall. There was also a store that sold a surprisingly good imitation of his painting of a kingfisher on

Pa-ta Shan-jen

a lotus for only 100RMB, or $20. Finn bought a copy of the painting, and I bought a copy of Pa-ta Shan-jen's collected poems.

The poems were collected from the inscriptions he wrote on his paintings. This was a unique characteristic of Chinese art, and invariably annoyed Westerners who preferred paintings to be simply paintings. But Chinese painting was much more personal than Western art. A painting was often a gift. And a gift requires a message. What better message than a poem? I opened the book at random, and there was one titled "Written on Kingfishers and Lotuses": "I've heard the wings of a king-fisher pair / grow longer when they fly home / how then do mindless clouds / float above lotuses day after day. 側聞雙翠鳥／歸飛翼已長／日日雲無心／那得蓮花上."

Few Chinese painters painted with such a free and fun-loving brush as Pa-ta Shan-jen. Anyone who sees his paintings for the first time can't help but be captivated. The nicest part of Blue Cloud Garden, though, wasn't its collection of paintings in the memorial hall or its store, but its garden wall. We had never seen anything quite like it. The wall undulated through the eastern part of the garden along a covered walkway for about forty meters. It was a wall with a dozen differently shaped windows that looked onto the surrounding ponds and rice fields. And on both sides of the wall were Pa-ta Shan-jen's paintings and poems carved into stone. It was a wonderful way to view his work, much better than turning the pages of a book.

We lingered there all afternoon in Pa-ta Shan-jen's old garden. It was impossible to leave. We were practically the only visitors, except for a few couples who came to be alone. There was also a teahouse, and once we had seen what there was to see, we sat down and ordered a pot of Iron Goddess. It was the perfect place to catch up on our journals. We tried to write every day. Our memories were bad, and every day we saw so much. After the first pot lost its flavor, we ordered a second pot. We were in no hurry. Our train didn't leave until nearly midnight, and we stayed until the caretaker said it was time to close. On our way out, we stopped to pay our respects at Pa-ta Shan-jen's grave. The tomb was in the corner of the garden flanked by two 400-year-old camphor trees that were just getting started when Pa-ta Shan-jen moved here rather than serve a government he didn't respect.

Pa-ta Shan-jen's grave

If we had been a little more ambitious, we might have also visited the grave of one of China's greatest writers. His name was T'ang Hsien-tsu (1550–1616). The Chinese like to call him their Shakespeare, and the comparison isn't misplaced. When it comes to drama, T'ang was the best. His seventeenth-century novel *Peony Pavilion* is still considered one of the great works of Chinese literature. He spent most of his life in his hometown of Linchuan, and he was buried there. Linchuan is only a hundred kilometers southeast of Nanchang, but we didn't want to spend half the day on the road—which is what it would have taken to go there and back. We were satisfied we made the right decision to drink tea instead.

From Pa-ta Shan-jen's memorial hall, we walked back to the main road and took the next bus back to our hotel, where we had left our bags with the concierge earlier that morning. We still had time on our hands, and we hadn't eaten all day, so we walked across the street and ordered dinner at one of the stalls that took over the sidewalk when the sun went down.

The trouble with ordering food on a sidewalk is that there isn't usually a menu. And we were feeling so good, we ordered without asking the price. It's a mistake I keep making no matter how many times I've traveled in China. But on this occasion we were distracted by a prostitute who sat down at our table and joined us for a beer. After dinner, when we asked for the bill, it turned out to be more than twice what it should have been. We should have chastised ourselves for forgetting to ask the prices, but on this occasion we decided to try something different. We refused to pay and told the owner that she should call the police. We got up to leave and told her that when the police came we would be in the bar across the street. Of course we were bluffing. And of course it was our fault for not asking the price in the first place. But we still had several hours to kill, and we thought we might as well experiment with the boundaries of negotiation. It was a unique situation, but it didn't last nearly as long as we had hoped. The owner immediately settled for half of what she had asked, and we even parted on friendly terms, promising to return on our next visit to the dubious destination of Nanchang.

But we weren't bluffing about visiting the bar across the street. We hadn't had any whiskey since we began our trip, so we decided to splurge. We walked into the lobby of the five-star Kiangsi Guesthouse, then into the hotel bar and bought each other shots. It was only Red Label, but we felt rich. Finally, we walked back to our hotel and collected our bags, and hauled ourselves to the train station. Since we had soft sleeper tickets, we were entitled to hang out in the VIP lounge, which we did until the express came and carried us through the night and dropped us off in Chingtechen at six o'clock the next morning. It was too early to do any sightseeing, and we were too tired anyway. We indulged ourselves by checking into the Chingtechen Guesthouse, where a triple cost an incredible 200RMB, or $40. Somehow we didn't mind. We felt we deserved a break. We went up to our room and went back to sleep. In fact, we spent the whole morning in bed. We felt as if we had finally discovered the proper way to travel.

磁器 墨水

10. Porcelain & Ink

It was almost noon when we woke up. Since we were in Chingtechen, the porcelain capital of China—if not the world—and only had the afternoon to see the sights, we asked the clerk at the front desk about hiring a guide. He directed us to the hotel's travel service, and five minutes later we not only had a guide, we had a van. The combination

Preparing clay for throwing

wasn't cheap, at 150RMB for a half-day tour, but we were feeling very self-indulgent after our morning nap. Only the unemployed and self-indulgent can take a morning nap.

In America, we call porcelain "china." And we don't use it for everyday meals. Assuming we have any, we only take it out for special occasions. Obviously, it's called "china" because it comes from China. And if it comes from China, the chances are it comes from Chingtechen. The potters and kilns of Chingtechen have been producing porcelain since the third century. Back then, though, it wasn't so highly prized. Utensils made of bronze or jade were preferred at court. In fact, when it first appeared, porcelain was called "imitation jade."

Despite its poor-man's-jade beginnings, porcelain was soon seen as capable of a much greater range of colors and designs, and it was far easier to produce than utensils made of bronze or jade. By the seventh century, porcelain, or *tz'u-ch'i*, as the Chinese call it, began appearing at court, and by the eleventh century, one Sung dynasty emperor ordered that he would use nothing except Chingtechen porcelain. As it happened, that Sung emperor's reign title was Ching-te, and all the porcelain produced for use at his court was stamped on the bottom with those words. Hence, the town that had previously been known as Hsinping and later Changnan became known as Chingtechen, or Chingte Township.

Once we finished lunch, we began our tour with a visit to the site of Chingtechen's most famous Sung kiln. It was four kilometers east of town and was called Hutien. This is where China's ubiquitous blue-and-white ware, the ware that became known in the West as "china," was first produced. The Istanbul Museum has a collection of blue-and-white ware from the Hutien kiln dating back to the thirteenth century. That was when Genghis Khan and his successors ruled all of Asia, including China and Turkey, and the Mongols preferred Chingtechen's blue-and-white ware. Prior to that, the Hutien kiln was better known for its ivory-white and pale-blue glazes, which the Chinese preferred to the more ostentatious blue-and-white. But a customer is a customer. And the customer is always right, especially if the customer is Genghis Khan.

The kiln, of course, was no longer extant, but we wanted to visit the

Kiln smokestack

Wood curing for use in kilns

site. In recent years, historians have picked through the ruins and have dug up enough fine pieces to fill a small museum. We thought they might have missed something. After parking along the roadside, we walked over to the kiln site and started looking among the ruins. But whenever we bent down to pick something up, our guide stopped us. She said picking up even the smallest shard was illegal. It was a protected site, she said.

Since there wasn't anything to see at the kiln site other than rubble (rubble we couldn't touch) we walked across the street to the museum. In addition to the porcelain bowls and cups and vases unearthed at the kiln site, the collection included the tools used by the potters who made the bowls and cups and vases. The displays also included models of the different kinds of kilns at Hutien. Their names suggested their shapes: the calabash, the horseshoe, and the dragon kiln. The dragon kiln was especially interesting. It was a long brick tunnel built on the slope of a hillside. Our guide told us there were still several dragon kilns in the Chingtechen area, but they weren't used very often, as they require a lot of wood. We laughed at the thought of fire-breathing dragons eating wood.

After we had seen what there was to see, our guide took us to the other side of town. Near the end of the seventeenth century, the city's kilns were relocated west of Chingtechen near Chushan, or Pearl Hill, and the kilns around Pearl Hill then became the center of the city's porcelain production. According to our guide, they operated day and night and gave Chingtechen its nickname, "the town of thunder and lightning," because of the glow and roar of the kiln fires.

In recent years, production has moved away from Pearl Hill, and the city's porcelain is now produced at more than 300 factories spread throughout the county. The kilns and workshops of Pearl Hill that we visited were more of a living museum than a center of production. As we walked through the area, the potters who worked there showed us the entire production process as it took place during the Ming dynasty. While the rest of the town's kilns used oil or gas or electricity, the Ming-dynasty style kilns at Pearl Hill still used fir grown locally then air cured for at least a year.

We even had a chance to make a pot ourselves. We weren't very good at it. Our pots weren't even round. But it was fun to feel the clay. It was the clay, after all, that made Chingtechen what it was. It was first discovered forty kilometers southwest of town on Kaoling Hill, and the clay was named after the hill. When it was first introduced to the West, Westerners spelled the name *kaolin*, and they've called it kaolin clay ever since. When our guide told us that Chingtechen's 300 factories produced over 300 million pieces of porcelain every year, we asked how much longer the clay would last. Surely, we thought, it would run out soon. She said not to worry. At the current level of production, Chingtechen had enough kaolin clay to last another 340 years. Obviously, Kaoling must be more of a mountain than a hill.

Our guide also offered to take us to one of the factories. She said we could paint and glaze our own vases or bowls, and the factory would fire them and send them to us in America. We turned down the factory tour in favor of visiting one of the government-run shops. We wanted to take home something of higher quality than something we made. Unfortunately, I'm still waiting for a blue-and-white bowl I bought for

200RMB from the state-run Chingtechen Arts & Crafts Company at No. 27 Chushan Road. Let the buyer beware.

That was all we had time for. We were tired, and our next destination was 200 kilometers to the east in the neighboring province of Anhui. But when our guide took us to the train station to buy tickets, there were no seats, soft or hard, on any train heading east—not for that day, the next day, or the day after that. We didn't feel like standing on a train for 200 kilometers. We wanted seats. The alternative was to take a bus. At least we would have seats. But we would also have to listen to the air-horn that drivers use at the slightest provocation. However, one rule I've learned traveling in China is that if there's a front door, there's also a back door. When we went back outside and told our guide about the non-availability of tickets, she went back inside with our money and came out a few minutes later. She not only got us tickets, she got us soft sleeper berths. They were berths on the same train we arrived on the day before. The day before, we got off half-asleep. The next morning, we got on half-awake. But at least we didn't have to stay awake. We had berths, and as soon as we got on, we stretched out and went back to sleep. Every once in a while, we looked out the window as the train snaked its way past mountains that had been deforested and replanted with tea. Everyone was growing tea. Apparently there wasn't enough money in trees. Eight hours after we got on in Chingtechen, we got off in Anhui province in the town of Shehsien.

Not many trains stopped in Shehsien, and not many tourists got off when they did. Anyone who came to this part of Anhui was usually here to see the scenic splendor of Huangshan. Huangshan was also on our itinerary, but not that day. There were some things we wanted to see in Shehsien first. In former times, Shehsien was the administrative center for the region and was called Huichou. And Huichou produced two of the four treasures of the scholar's studio, the first of which was ink.

According to legend, Shehsien was where ink was first produced 2,800 years ago. During the Chou dynasty, a man from Shehsien formed charcoal and glutinous rice into balls that he then ground on a stone, to which he added water. Most of the major improvements in the production of ink

Artisan adding a design to a bowl

since then had also occurred in the Shehsien area, including the charcoal and oil-soot inksticks of Li T'ing-kuei. Back in the T'ang dynasty, Li's inksticks were worth more than gold, as were those of his recent successor, Hu K'ai-wen. The factory that Hu's descendants set up in Shehsien was still in operation, although it is no longer a family-run business. It has been taken over by the state. Still, its reputation hasn't diminished. Orders have continued to come from calligraphers around the world. Hence, the first thing we did when we arrived in Shehsien was hire a taxi to take us there.

Usually visiting a factory in China required going through bureaucratic channels. But we didn't have time for that and thought we would try the direct approach. We told the gate guard at the factory we were poets and wanted to see how ink was made. Of course, it must have sounded silly. It certainly did to us. But apparently we weren't the only people who tried the direct approach. Instead of turning us away, the guard pointed us toward the administration building, and a few minutes later we were talking to the director. He explained to us that the secret behind the fame of Shehsien ink was the region's mist. That sounded ludicrous. But he said the mist made for superior pine trees, which made for superior wood, which made for superior charcoal, which made for superior soot, which made for superior ink.

He then led us through the workshops and showed us how the soot from burning pine charcoal or tung oil was collected from the bottoms of huge curved metal lids that were suspended over the fires. The soot was then combined with glue made from animal hides and other ingredients, such as ground pearls, to give the ink a certain amount of luster, and drops of musk oil, to give the ink its distinctive perfume. Once these and other secret ingredients were added, the ink was then kneaded and pounded as if making bread. When it was finally the right consistency, the black dough was then put into wooden molds. But it was only allowed to stay in the molds for a few hours. It was taken out of the molds while it was still pliable, then air-dried indoors. The director said if the inksticks were dried outside in the sun or the wind, they would crack. Finally, he led us into the last set of workshops where hundreds of girls were busy painting gold leaf onto the designs that had been

Artisan adding gold leaf to an inkstick

impressed onto the inksticks by the molds. Before leaving, we naturally stopped in the factory store and bought enough inksticks to keep us and our calligraphy friends happy for years.

Ink, though, is only one of the four treasures of every Chinese scholar's or artist's studio. They also need paper and brushes. Shehsien was not particularly famous for either of these. But it was famous for the fourth of the four treasures, namely inkstones, the stones on which calligraphers and artists grind their ink.

After thanking the director for his personal tour of the town's most famous inkstick factory, we returned to our taxi and headed for the town's most famous inkstone factory. From the eastern outskirts of town, we drove back through the old part of Shehsien then across a tributary of the Hsin-an River to the new part of town and the Shehsien Inkstone Factory. We weren't expected here either, and it was already late in the day. But once again the guard at the gate called the director's office on our behalf. The director was busy, but he was kind enough to ask the factory supervisor to show us around. And a few minutes later we began our tour.

Although the Shehsien Inkstone Factory was just as famous as the Hu K'ai-wen Ink Factory, there were no secrets to the production process, as there were with ink. But we soon found out that not all stones are created equal, and the stone of choice is slate. According to our guide, slate has a smooth, dense grain, which makes grinding ink easier and also prevents the ink from being absorbed into the stone. The reason, she said, for the concentration of inkstone production in Shehsien was because of its stones and also because of its artisans. The best stones, she said, come from Lungweishan, or Dragon Tail Mountain. Even though the mountain is a hundred kilometers to the southwest, it has always been within the jurisdiction of Shehsien. And because Shehsien is the administrative center for the region, it has also attracted a large number of skilled artisans. Not only are the stones of Shehsien famous, so is the carving.

After telling us about the history of Shehsien inkstones, the supervisor led us into the workshop area. The factory didn't produce your ordinary, run-of-the-mill stones. Its yearly output was only 20,000 stones, and it only employed 200 workers. That averaged out to 100 stones per worker

Artisan carving an inkstone

per year. But no worker was in charge of the whole process. Each stone passed from worker to worker as it went through a number of different stages of refinement. During the final carving, each stone passed through the hands of ten different artisans as the carving and grinding and polishing became finer and finer.

After visiting the workshops, we finally went into the factory store. The supervisor told us that most of the designs were developed by the factory but anyone who wanted to order something special was welcome to do so. I saw no need to design my own stone. I saw one that was already perfect. It was carved in the shape of a lotus leaf and was supported on the bottom by snails. And on top, a frog peered out from the tiny pond where the ink collected after grinding. It came inside an equally lovely rosewood box, also carved in the shape of a lotus leaf. When I bought it, though, I felt torn. It was so beautiful I knew I couldn't use it myself. I would have to give it to my wife. I already had an inkstone at home, and it was good enough for me. My calligraphy didn't warrant a lotus leaf. But my wife's did.

My calligraphy teacher once told me there was another treasure of the Chinese studio beyond the basic four of ink, inkstone, paper, and brush. My teacher's name was Chuang Yen, and he was one of the most famous calligraphers in Taiwan at the time. He had retired from his post as deputy curator of Taiwan's Palace Museum, so he had time to teach a few students, and I was fortunate to be one of them.

In those days (the seventies and eighties), I had to go to Hong Kong every six months to renew my tourist visa, and I asked him if I could bring back any Mainland products for him, perhaps some ink or brushes. Until 1987, people in Taiwan weren't allowed to go to China or to bring back anything made in the Mainland. The only thing Chuang Yen wanted was a bottle of sorghum spirits known as Tachuchiu. When I asked him why, he told me he did his best work when he got up around four o'clock in the morning and washed away the night with a cup or two of white lightning. And Tachuchiu was his favorite. Not many people know about the fifth treasure, but I don't think Chuang Yen would mind if I shared his secret.

黄山 九花山
11. Huangshan & Chiuhuashan

Just as the sun was going down, we boarded a bus and said good-bye to Shehsien. An hour later, we said hello to Tunhsi. Tunhsi is the gateway to Huangshan, China's most spectacular mountain. That was our next destination, but it was still more than an hour away, and it was too late to try shortening the distance. We checked into a hotel near the bus station, then went looking for a place to eat in the old part of town.

Finally Believing Peak

In addition to serving as the gateway to Huangshan, Tunhsi is also a gateway to the Sung dynasty. The city government rebuilt one of the streets in the old part of town as it might have looked a thousand years ago. While the architecture might have been reminiscent of the Sung dynasty, that was the limit of the resemblance. We must have walked past a hundred old-style shops selling the same new-style antiques and tourist souvenirs. We didn't see anything of interest, nothing that matched the inksticks and inkstones of Shehsien. One store we at least went inside was the Tungtejen Pharmacy. It had been doing business on this street for over 200 years. The aroma of the herbs drew us in. But, as fascinating as it was, we weren't feeling ill. We were, however, feeling hungry and tried a Sung-dynasty dumpling place that wasn't bad. I don't remember the name, but we were easily satisfied and went to bed early.

We went to bed early because we wanted to be on the first bus of the day to Huangshan. It left at 6:30, and we wanted to get an early start. Huangshan is, after all, one of the biggest tourist destinations in China. It is China's most photographed mountain and also China's most painted mountain. In fact, two of the country's most famous landscape schools were centered there: the Huangshan School and the Hsin-an School, both of which began there more than 300 years ago. They represented two different ways of painting—with a minimum of ink and simpler brushwork in the case of the Hsin-an School—but they shared the same source of inspiration: Huangshan. Anyone who sees a collection of Chinese landscape paintings from the Ch'ing dynasty is probably seeing examples of these two schools. Though their brushwork and their use of color differed, both schools were inspired by the mountain's cloud-wrapped peaks and pine-studded crags. This was what we were also hoping to see (but not in a painting).

Strangely, the bus we got on was nearly empty. This was because it wasn't a regular bus; it was a tour bus on its way back to Huangshan to pick up passengers it had delivered there the previous day. As we left Tunhsi behind, we followed a road along a river and began passing two-story farmhouses whose architecture hadn't changed for hundreds of years: the distinctive white walls and black-tiled roofs of Anhui.

Once again, we couldn't help noticing that the hillsides had been deforested and replanted with tea. Our driver confirmed our suspicion that
the deforestation had led to floods. He also told us that villagers in the
Huangshan area divided work differently from those in other parts of
China. He said the men stayed home and took care of the children,
while the women worked in the fields and tended the tea. We found
that hard to believe. But we didn't have a chance to find out if it was
true or not.

As we got closer, we could see Huangshan in the distance. It looked
like any other mountain. It was big, but not spectacular. Just another
mountain. That was what people had thought for centuries. They had
no idea what was on top. In fact, until the last century, Huangshan
wasn't known outside of the art schools centered there and a few rare
travelers who hiked to the summit. But not long after the Nationalists
established their capital in Nanking in 1927, they built a road halfway
up the mountain, and word soon spread.

I should also note that it wasn't always called Huangshan. It used
to be called Yishan, *yi* being another word for "black." I'm not sure
why. It didn't look black. Gray, yes, but not black. In any case, when
Emperor Hsuan-tsung passed by the mountain in the eighth century,
he decided to change the name to Huangshan, or Yellow Mountain, in
honor of Huang-ti, the Yellow Emperor, who reportedly completed his
course of Taoist training there. Hsuan-tsung, too, had no idea what was
on top. But we did. We had seen photos—and paintings.

Finally, ninety minutes after leaving Tunhsi, we arrived at the foot
of the mountain at a place called Tangkou. After dropping our gear
at a cheap hotel near the bus station, we took a shuttle bus halfway
up the mountain to Yunku Temple. The temple was long gone but not
the name. It sounded nice: Cloud Valley Temple. It was just past eight
o'clock in the morning when we arrived, but there must have been close
to five hundred people already in line. They were all waiting for the
cable car.

People who visit Huangshan have their choice: the cable car or the
trail, and both begin at the former site of Yunku Temple. The trail is 7.5

Huangshan peak in a sea of clouds

kilometers and takes three hours to walk. The cable car takes ten minutes. The wait, though, can last hours. In our case, it lasted two hours, which was still better—we thought— than hiking to the top. At least we wouldn't be exhausted when we got there.

Finally, our turn came, and up we went. Even if the cable car was a bit crowded, it was a glorious ascent. Ten minutes later, we were standing just below the northeast corner of the summit. One of the first things we noticed when we got out of the cable car was a sign saying that smoking was only allowed in designated areas and discarding trash was prohibited. This was good news. When Steve and I first visited the mountain several years earlier, the place was littered with trash. This time, we had to look hard to find anything, even a cigarette butt. If any mountain deserved this sort of respect, it was Huangshan.

Everyone who has ever been there agrees: it's the most spectacular mountain in China. But standing there awestruck was not the way to enjoy the mountain, a mountain that's an infinitely long scroll with a thousand views. From the cable car terminal, we followed the main trail of stone steps for about ten minutes, then we turned onto a side trail that led to a place called Shihhsinfeng, or Finally Believing Peak. The view is one of the most photographed and painted scenes on Huangshan. Huangshan is famous for two things: its rock spires, barren of everything except a few gnarled pines, and its sea of clouds that often obscure the rock spires and gnarled pines, leaving only a single protruding pinnacle or branch. Shihhsinfeng is famous for both, and both were waiting for us.

Once we reached the overlook, we just stood there watching the scene change as clouds drifted in and out. It wasn't simply one scene. It was as if the stage manager of a play was changing the scenery. We could have stood there all day, but our tour of the summit was just beginning. We retraced our steps to the main trail and continued skirting the north side of the mountain. As we did, we were surprised to pass several hotels. We weren't planning to spend the night, but we went inside one and inquired. Even the smallest, simplest of rooms without a view cost over a hundred dollars a night. We could think of better places to spend our money and returned to the trail.

Huangshan pines

As we did, we had to stop every few minutes. Every few minutes revealed another spectacular view. Also, every few minutes, we needed to catch our breaths. It was the elevation: The cable car from Yunku Temple transported us from 900 meters, which was already fairly high, to 1,700 meters, which was much higher than we were used to. Where I was living in Hong Kong was ten meters above sea level, and where Finn and Steve lived near Seattle was less than 100 meters above the same ocean.

And so we huffed and puffed and *oohed* and *aahed* our way from the northeast to the northwest corner of the mountain. Finally, around noon, we arrived at a place called Paiyunlou, or Cloudbreak Pavilion. This was where people came to watch the sunset. There was also a hotel here, and we stopped long enough to have a simple lunch. It had to be simple, because everything was so expensive. All the food had to be brought up the mountain on someone's back or in a cable car.

Afterwards, we followed the trail along the western side of the summit to the south side. As we did, we hiked past a side trail that led to Feilaishih, or Rock That Flew Here. It seems like every mountain in China has a Feilaishih, perched as if it would blow over in a strong wind. But Huangshan's Rock That Flew Here was the biggest one we had seen. We watched people stand next to it and try to push it over. Lucky for them, it didn't budge.

We left it where it was and continued on to the weather station, where the trail divided and where we had a choice. We could return to the hotels on the north side of the summit and the cable car that brought us up. Or we could continue along the west side of the summit to the cable car on the south side, and that was what we did. We were glad we did: the views were worth the effort. And the crowds thinned out. We often found ourselves alone, which rarely happens on the north side of the summit. Along the way, we passed by several small temples that had been converted into hostels, but we were determined to get down the mountain before dark and didn't stop.

Along the way, there was also a side trail to Lienhuafeng, or Lotus Peak. It was Huangshan's highest peak at nearly 1,900 meters. We thought about it, but we didn't think about it long. Soon after that, we came to the mountain's famous Welcoming Pine. We had seen pictures of it everywhere in China, especially in hotel lobbies, where it welcomes guests to spend the night. It's the most famous pine tree in China, and seeing the real thing was worth all the ups and downs of the trail. We sat down on a stone bench and took in the view. We sat there so long we began to get cold and had to put on our jackets. It was getting late. Fortunately, we didn't have far to go, and we reached the Yuping cable car with an hour to spare—it stopped operating at sunset.

One of the advantages of coming down the mountain via the Yuping, or Jade Screen, cable car is that it ends at a hot-spring hotel. We couldn't resist. It wasn't cheap, but for 30RMB a person we spent an hour soaking away our muscles' memory of the trail. It didn't take away all the soreness, but it was a great way to end the day. After our baths, we still had to take the shuttle bus back down the mountain to our crummy hotel, which seemed especially crummy after the day on Huangshan. But once we were asleep it didn't matter. We weren't done with mountains, and we planned to sleep on one the next night.

Our next destination was Chiuhuashan. We were going from China's most scenic mountain to one of its most sacred. The two mountains weren't that far apart as the crow flew. Unfortunately, we weren't crows. We had to take the bus, and there was only one a day from Tangkou. It left every morning at 7:30, and we made sure we were on it. It began its daily journey by winding its way north through a long valley to Taiping Reservoir. After waiting for half an hour at the ferry, we crossed the reservoir, then drove through a countryside of rice fields and hillsides of tea before finally winding our way up Chiuhuashan. Six hours after we left, we were there.

The name Chiuhuashan means Nine Flower Mountain. Its old name was Chiutzushan, or Nine Son Mountain, after the sons of a family that first settled here. Then one day 1,250 years ago, the poet Li Pai visited the mountain. Li got drunk with some friends and wrote a poem in which he praised the mountain's nine flower-like peaks, and the name Nine Flower Mountain stuck. Actually, Chiuhuashan has more than nine peaks, but in ancient China, the word for "nine" also meant "many."

Despite giving the mountain its name, Li Pai is not someone people think about when they come here. At some point during our bus ride, I took out a picture of Ti-tsang Bodhisattva to show to Finn and Steve. One of our fellow passengers saw us looking at it, and suddenly everyone wanted to see it. So we passed it around. It turned out we were on a bus full of pilgrims. Ti-tsang is the bodhisattva who vowed to save all the beings in Hell, and Chiuhuashan was his home.

Among the dozens of bodhisattvas venerated by Chinese Buddhists, Kuan-yin is number-one. But Ti-tsang is a close second. After all, everyone is going to need his help sooner or later. Actually, the two form a perfect pair. Kuan-yin is usually portrayed as a woman who holds a vase of life-giving water, while Ti-tsang is portrayed as a monk who holds a staff he uses to pry open the gates of Hell. Kuan-yin helps those who are alive, while Ti-tsang helps those who aren't.

Chiuhuashan is said to be his home because Ti-tsang first manifested himself here as a Korean monk who came to the mountain in the T'ang dynasty. His name wasn't Ti-tsang. It was Chin Ch'iao-chueh.

But he made the same vow Ti-tsang made to save all the beings in Hell, and while the Korean monk was still alive, people started calling him Ti-tsang. And in the centuries following the monk's death, Chiuhuashan became venerated as his residence.

Chinese Buddhists venerate four such mountains as homes of their religion's heroes, the ones they call bodhisattvas, which are beings who vow to forgo nirvana in order to save others. Buddhism recognizes hundreds of bodhisattvas, but four are revered above the rest, and their places of residence are the principal destinations of Buddhist pilgrims in China. The residence of Manjusri, or Wen-shu, the Bodhisattva of Great Wisdom, is on Wutaishan in North China; the residence of Samantabadra, or P'u-hsien, the Boddhisattva of Skillful Means, is on Omeishan in West China; the residence of Avalokitesvara, or Kuan-yin, the Bodhisattva of Great Compassion, is on Putuoshan off the east coast of China; and Chiuhuashan, the southern member of Buddhism's four sacred mountains, is the residence of Ksitigarbha, or Ti-tsang, the Bodhisattva of Great Vows.

After six hours on a hard-seat bus, we were glad to be there. Steve and I had been to Chiuhuashan two years earlier and had stayed at one of the monasteries. We decided to see if we could stay there again. From the bus station, we walked past the long row of incense sellers and trinket shops and food stalls that catered to pilgrims. After a few minutes, we came to Chantanlin, Sandalwood Forest Temple. We walked inside, and a minute later we found the abbot. He recognized us, and he welcomed us back. His name was Hui-shen, and he showed us to a room next to a small garden at the back of the temple. After leaving us alone for a few minutes, he returned.

Hui-shen was short and wiry. I never got a chance to find out his age, but he was probably in his fifties. He wasn't interested in small talk. He sat down next to my bed on the only chair in the room and spent the next two hours doing what he could to help us see through the world of red dust. Steve and I began by telling Hui-shen we had met several hermits during our previous trip and we planned to visit them again.

Hui-shen said that hermits were no big deal and that most of them weren't worth visiting. He said, "If you want to become a buddha, you first have to become a human being. Only by becoming a human being, can you become a buddha. Buddhas don't exist outside this world. Enlightenment comes from realizing the true nature of suffering. How can you experience human suffering if you live in a cave or in a hut in the mountains? You have to live in the world of human beings. Why do you want to visit hermits?"

We told him we liked hermits. We liked their simple lives, and we liked the way they smiled. We also liked listening to Hui-shen. He was determined to teach us something, and he kept poking his finger into our sides to make sure we understood. Just in case we didn't, he wrote everything down. I still have the backs of a dozen envelopes and scraps of paper he left in our room covered with his summaries of the Dharma.

Finally, another monk came in and called him away. A group of pilgrims wanted to pay for a funeral service. Just in case their departed loved ones went down instead of up, pilgrims come to Chiuhuashan to ask Ti-tsang for special consideration. In fact, funeral services are the main source of income for nearly all the temples on the mountain, and most of the monks and nuns on Chiuhuashan spend part of every day chanting scriptures to help relieve the suffering of the departed as well as the suffering of those they left behind.

Even though Hui-shen didn't think hermits deserved our attention, much less our time, Steve and I met a nun living in a hut the first time we visited Chiuhuashan, and we wanted to visit her again. We called her the Tiger Lady. She didn't tell us her real name. The trail to her hut began just up from the bus station next to Chihyuan Temple. The first part was easy enough, although it was straight up. When we reached the ridge that encircled the pilgrimage center below, we turned left onto a dirt trail that came and went. After a few false starts, we finally found the trail that led down the other side of the mountain. A small sign confirmed that this was, indeed, the trail to Tiger Cave that Steve and I had followed two years earlier. We followed it again, and a few minutes later we were there. Next to the cave was a mud-brick hut with whitewashed walls. It was the Tiger Lady's home. We saw her working in her garden and yelled "*Omitofo.*" She stood up and looked puzzled.

Tiger Cave and Tiger Lady's hut

She was a Buddhist nun, and for the past ten years she had been living next to the cave. The first time we visited her, she showed us tiger tracks in her garden. She said she only saw the tiger a few times, but she heard it almost every night. When we asked her if she remembered us, she just shrugged. She said a couple foreigners visited her a few years back, but it wasn't us. We asked her how the young monk was doing. When we'd visited her before, she told us a young monk was living in a nearly inaccessible niche farther down the cliff. He was completely devoted to his meditation practice, and she told us he didn't have anything to eat. So we gave her 100RMB and asked her to buy him some food. She said the young monk left a few months ago. We asked her if she remembered us giving her money to help take care of him. She said she remembered a couple foreigners giving her some money, but it wasn't us.

She led us inside Tiger Cave, and we paid our respects at the shrine for the monk who lived here 1,500 years ago and for the tiger that kept him company. Then she led us up onto the rocks above the cave. She jumped onto a ledge like a cat and motioned for us to follow. We struggled up.

Master Hui-shen at Chantanlin Temple

While we all crouched on the ledge next to a huge boulder, she said this was the best spot to view the rest of the mountain. It was. Across the neighboring gorge, two waterfalls hung in space. The rest was all clouds and forest and rocky spires. In the distance, we could see the trail that pilgrims took to the main peak. The peak looked far away, and the trail to the top must have consisted of several thousand steps. Hiking to the Tiger Lady's hut was enough for us.

When we went back down to her hut, she turned away to show us something, and we slipped some money under a plate. She wanted to show us a picture of Ti-tsang. She said it was very special and had been blessed by a Tibetan lama who visited her. We said, "*Omitofo*." She also poured us some tea and gave us some candy. We drank the tea but left the candy. Finally, we told her we had to go. We said good-bye and retraced our steps back to the pilgrimage center.

It was time for us to pay our respects to Ti-tsang. We walked past the temple where we were staying to a set of steps that led up the mountain. A couple hundred steps later, we reached Joushen Paodien, or Material Body Hall. It was where the Korean monk's body was kept. It was inside a pagoda in the middle of a shrine hall. The monk in charge told us that the body was still in perfect condition. When we asked him how he knew, he said the monks take it out the last day of the seventh month every year and give it a sponge bath—in private. We then lit some incense and joined dozens of other pilgrims circumambulating the pagoda.

This was the principal stop on the Chiuhuashan pilgrim trail. The trail continued on another five or six kilometers and eventually up a long, steep flight of stone steps to the top of the next ridge. On a clear day, we were told, Huangshan is visible to the east and the Yangtze to the west. And if you get tired along the way, sedan chair porters are glad to help you out. But we had seen enough. We walked back down to our monastic lodging and met Master Hui-shen again. When we told him we would be leaving the next morning, he wrote down one last thing for us to keep in mind: "A deluded mind is like ice. An enlightened mind is like water. It flows through the valley of life, unattached." All we could think of to say was, "*Omitofo*."

李白

12. Li Pai

We were truly sad to leave Chantanlin and Master Hui-shen. He tried his best to see that we left the mountain a little wiser than when we arrived. But it was time to leave. As we walked down the gauntlet of shops catering to pilgrims and tourists, we were puzzled when we noticed that they all sold statues of Kuan-yin, the Bodhisattva of

Place where Li Pai embraced the moon

Compassion. Ti-tsang was nowhere in sight. Chiuhuashan was Ti-tsang's home. Why no statues? And what was Kuan-yin doing here? Her home was on an island in the East China Sea. We thought about it and concluded that Chinese Buddhists prefer to have a statue of the Goddess of Mercy at home. Who wants to be reminded of Hell?

And so we said good-bye to Ti-tsang, at least for the time being, and left on the seven o'clock bus to Nanking—not that we were going that far. Four hours later, we got off in Hsuancheng. The reason we got off there was paper. We had already visited the factories in Shehsien that produced the most famous inksticks and inkstones in China. Paper was the third of the four treasures of the scholar's studio. And the paper known as *hsuan-chih* was the most famous of all. Since *hsuan-chih* was named after Hsuancheng, we figured this was the place to see it made. We figured wrong. When we asked at the bus station, we found out that all the *hsuan-chih* factories were near Chinghsien, fifty kilometers to the southwest. We were also told that they didn't welcome visitors. Their paper-making process was a secret. For the first time on our trip, we had to admit defeat.

From the bus station, it was a short walk to the train station, where we bought tickets on the next local heading north. While we were waiting on the platform, we met a man from Chinghsien. When he asked what we were doing there, we told him we were hoping to find out more about how *hsuan-chih* was made. He said he used to work at one of the factories, and he proceeded to tell us everything we ever wanted to know about his hometown's most famous product. The reason, he said, paper produced in Chinghsien was so famous, was the area's water. He said every factory was located near a mountain stream. To the water, they added elm and mulberry bark and rice straw. The hillsides around Chinghsien, he said, were covered with straw and bark most of the year. It had to be bleached for months before it could be used. Also, every kind of paper required special ingredients, many of which were secret. One ingredient he mentioned that caught us by surprise was kiwi juice.

Paper from these ingredients, he said, was first produced in Chinghsien during the Han dynasty nearly 2,000 years ago. By the end of the T'ang, 1,000 years ago, it was the favorite paper of China's leading calligraphers and artists. Since then, numerous grades and varieties had been developed. And nowadays, no calligrapher or artist would settle for anything less than *hsuan-chih*, which was produced, we were sad to say, in Chinghsien, not in Hsuancheng, where we stood waiting for our train.

The northbound finally came, and two hours later, we were the only passengers who got off in Tangtu. It was a funny name. It meant Stuck in the Mud. But it was a sunny day, and there was no rain in sight. After asking directions, we walked across a bridge to a place where buses passed by and and caught one headed for Huangchih, which was about thirty kilometers to the southeast. Thirty minutes later, halfway there, we got off at the grave of Li Pai.

When Chinese rank their poets, they always put Tu Fu and Li Pai at the top. We had already visited Tu Fu's weed-covered grave in the countryside north of Changsha. Li Pai's grave had fared better, probably because of its proximity to Nanking—which had been the capital of a number of southern dynasties. The grave was in a park-like setting near the foot of Chingshan and surrounded by a long white wall. When he died in 762, Li Pai was buried several kilometers to the west on Lungshan. But 150 years later, his remains were moved to Chingshan in accordance with his wishes. I'm not sure why it took so long.

It was a big place. There were ponds and waterways and bridges and exhibition halls and, of course, gardens. We spent half an hour strolling through the grounds and finally ended up at an exhibition hall at the rear of the park. One of the display cases contained several bricks from the original grave, and the walls were covered with paintings recounting the events of Li Pai's final years, when he was banished from the capital of Ch'ang-an and forced to drink his last cup of wine on the Yangtze.

Li Pai lived in the eighth century during an age when even peasants recited poems, and everyone who was anyone recited his. The rear of the exhibition hall opened up into an enclosed garden that surrounded his tomb—the same as Tu Fu's. We walked into the gar-

Li Pai's grave

den and sat down on one of the stone benches. I took out my copy of Li Pai's poems and read one to Finn and Steve. We were the only people there, so I didn't mind reading it out loud in Chinese then trying to translate it on the spot. While I was still working on the translation, two dozen Japanese filed in and lined up in front of Li Pai's grass-covered tomb. We didn't know what to think. It was like a military formation. Then one of them walked over to the tombstone and lit candles and incense. Once he rejoined his colleagues, they all began singing one of Li Pai's poems in unison. We found out later that they were members of a club in Japan that devoted itself to the study of T'ang poetry. But what was remarkable was that they sang his poems in the ancient T'ang dynasty dialect.

While the candles and incense were still burning, their leader ended their performance with a solo effort. He sang Li Pai's last poem titled "Song at the End of Life," in which Li Pai referred to himself as the mythical bird called the P'eng, which Chuang-tzu used at the beginning of his self-titled book to embody the spirit set free. In his poem, Li Pai also referred to the Chinese belief that the sun rose behind a huge tree and to the story that Confucius burst into tears when he heard that a unicorn had been captured.

> *Soaring above the world's horizon*
> *halfway to Heaven the P'eng's strength failed*
> *I had enough wind for ten thousand generations*
> *but my robe caught on the sunrise tree*
> *I leave it behind for whoever finds it*
> *Confucius is dead who'll cry for me*

As the singer reached that last line, his voiced cracked, and the strangest thing happened. The sky began to cry.

After everyone bowed in front of Li Pai's grave and filed out, we sat down on the grass in front of the grave in the rain. We had a beer, so we opened it, shared a swig, then poured the rest over Li Pai's tombstone. If there was one poet who liked to drink, it was Li Pai. Half the poems he

Japanese pilgrims at Li Pai's grave

Tomb containing Li Pai's hat and robe

left behind mention drinking. Here's one titled "Drinking with a Recluse in the Mountains":

> *We fill each other's cups where the wildflowers bloom*
> *one cup another cup and still one more*
> *I'm drunk and half-asleep when you get up to leave*
> *tomorrow if you come again don't forget your zither*

Too bad all we had was beer, and only one bottle. The rain didn't last long. About the time it stopped, we said good-bye to Li Pai and flagged down a bus going back to Tangtu. We got off at the same spot we got on and boarded the next bus heading north. Twenty kilometers later, we got off at the town of Tsaishih and walked to the nearby cliff of the same name. That was where the story was set that started circulating soon after Li Pai died. It went like this: one night when the moon was especially round, Li Pai rowed out into the Yangtze and dropped anchor below Tsaishih Cliff. As usual, he had a jug of wine with him, and before

Sculpture of Li Pa by Ch'ien Shao-wu

long he was drunk. Gazing at the moon's reflection in the water, he bent over and tried to embrace it. When he did, he fell into the river. Some say he drowned, while others say he was carried to Heaven on the back of a whale. Actually, the whale's appearance in this version isn't as far-fetched as it sounds. The region just south of Tsaishih Cliff is now a nature sanctuary for the Yangtze freshwater dolphin.

After watching the river traffic in the Yangtze for a while, we walked back via the hill that rose behind the cliff. Along the trail, we passed a huge stainless steel statue of Li Pai by the sculptor Ch'ien Shao-wu. It was a wonderful interpretation. Li Pai looked like a bird about to take off. In fact, an inscription by the sculptor noted that his interpretation was inspired by Li Pai's vision of himself as the mythic bird that began the Taoist work known as the *Chuang-tzu*: "In the North Sea there is a fish called K'un thousands of miles long. It rises out of the sea and turns into a bird called P'eng thousands of miles wide. Its wings are like clouds, and it soars 3,000 miles high before heading south toward the Lake of Heaven." The metaphor was apt. It was clearly on Li Pai's mind when he was dying. Just past the statue, we also stopped to visit another Li Pai grave. This one contained the poet's robe and hat. We bowed, just in case it contained more than that.

On our way back to the road, we also stopped to look inside the Li Pai Memorial Hall. The place was packed. A girl at the door said it was opening day of the First International Li Pai Conference. We looked around. Something was wrong. Everyone was sober. In Li Pai's honor, we bought a beer at a store outside the memorial hall and toasted him one more time, then caught the next bus heading north to Ma-anshan. Except for its steel mill, there wasn't much to see in Ma-anshan. Besides, it was already five o'clock. We stayed just long enough to eat a bowl of beef noodles at a restaurant near the train station, then we boarded the next train to Nanking. Nanking was as far north as we planned to go. After Nanking, it was all going to be downhill.

南京

13. Nanking

As our train pulled into Nanking, the sun was going down. It seemed like it was always going down when we arrived somewhere. Our days were so full. Since the next day was going to be full too, we decided to treat ourselves to something beyond our normal range of accommodations and checked into the Nanking Hotel, where a triple cost

Spirit way to Ming emperor's tomb

250RMB. At least we saved on dinner. We had noodles in Ma-anshan before we boarded the train. At the convenience store next to the hotel, we grabbed a few beers and a couple bags of peanuts and took them up to our room where we engaged in our favorite end-of-the-day pastimes: taking baths, washing our clothes, writing in our journals, and sleeping late the next morning. It was nine o'clock before we ventured forth to see the sights.

Nanking was the provincial capital of Kiangsu. But it wasn't like the other provincial capitals we had visited. Over the previous two thousand years, it had been the capital of a number of dynasties whose primary area of control was the southern half of China. In fact, the Chinese name for the city means Southern Capital. So there was a lot to see, and we only had a day. Our plan was to begin in the south and work our way north, back to our hotel before the sun went down again.

We began with a taxi ride all the way to Chuhuatai, or Chrysanthemum Terrace. It was a large park at the southernmost edge of the city, but we weren't there for the park. We told the driver to drop us off at the southeast corner. From the roadside, we followed a path into the park then turned off on a side trail where a sign pointed us toward our destination. Given the weeds along the trail, our destination didn't see many visitors. It felt strange. It was like discovering something the citizens of Nanking had forgotten. The trail soon led past a series of life-sized stone statues of animals and officials that constituted what the Chinese call a "spirit way." They, too, were knee-deep in weeds. We followed them until they ended at a small tomb. We walked over to make sure we had the right one (not that there were any other tombs that we could see). Sure enough, the tomb belonged to the King of Borneo.

When I first read about this tomb, I found it hard to believe that it was real. Yet there it was. The title and name of the country, however, were a bit misleading, if not mistaken. Nowadays we would call the man buried here the Sultan of Brunei. But King of Borneo was close enough, and it sounded much more exotic, which was, of course, why we made the effort to visit his tomb.

As for how the King got here, he arrived aboard Admiral Cheng Ho's fleet. The Chinese emperor sent Cheng on what remains the greatest diplomatic expedition in the history of the world—ancient or modern. Cheng sailed from Nanking all the way to Africa and back several times with a fleet of over 300 ships and a complement of 30,000 sailors and soldiers. One of the dignitaries he brought back was the King of Borneo, who died in Nanking before he had a chance to return home. That was why he was here. And that was why we were here. But once we found his tomb, we didn't linger. Our curiosity was easily satisfied.

We retraced our steps back to the road and flagged down another taxi and headed for another park. This one was called Yuhuatai, or Rain Flower Terrace. It was just south of the city's South Gate, better known as Chunghuamen. The terrace was actually a small hill in the middle of the park. This time we weren't looking for a tomb but for pebbles. The terrace was famous for the pebbles that lined a stream that flowed from a spring. The pebbles, so the story went, were once flowers that rained down on the hill when a monk preached here 1,500 years ago. They were, in fact, agates, and they came in all colors and sizes. On our way in, we passed several shops outside the park selling these crystallized flowers. They also sold them in bulk. A friend of mine in Hong Kong once bought one hundred kilos. When he got them home, he spread them underneath a coffee table in his living room and rubbed his feet in them for a daily foot massage.

We weren't looking to buy any, just look at them in their natural setting along the stream. Once again, our ignorance of the recent history of China surprised us. Before we reached the stream, we came to a memorial hall to the city's martyrs. We poked our heads inside. We thought we would just have a look then continue on to the pebbles. But once we started viewing the photographs and began reading about the two decades during which the Nationalists used Nanking as their capital, we lost interest in rain-flowers. The Nationalists executed more than 100,000 Communist sympathizers, right here at the base of Rain Flower Terrace. The enormity of such savagery was hard to comprehend. Why, we had to ask ourselves, do human beings do such things to each other? The answer, of course, is our infatuation with exercising power over each other, our insecurity and our mistrust—in a word, delusion. As we walked out of the memorial hall, we wondered if someone in the future might explain the pebbles of Rain Flower Terrace as the tears of Heaven. It would make more sense.

We walked back out of the park and continued north across the city's old moat, which was formed by a branch of the Chinhuai River, then past the imposing edifice of Chunghuamen Gate. This section of the river was said to be where the city began. And the gate was said to be the biggest city gate in all of China. But we kept going. We had something else in mind. A few blocks to the north, we turned off on a side street. A block later, we entered the Museum of the Taiping Rebellion.

The man who started the rebellion was Hung Hsiu-ch'uan. After reading several books about Christianity, Hung experienced a series of visions in which he was told that he was the brother of Jesus Christ. This was around 1830. On the basis of these visions, Hung founded a new religious sect and said that he had been ordained by Heaven to rid China of its Manchu overlords and to bring peace to all mankind: hence, the name of his movement: Taiping Tienkuo, the Kingdom of Heavenly Peace. The movement was welcomed by many Chinese who were tired of serving the Manchus, and within two decades the Taipings controlled large parts of South and Southwest China. In 1852, they established their capital in Nanking, and Hung became emperor of a new Taiping dynasty.

It was one of China's most interesting rebellions, coming as it did on the heels of the Opium War. And it probably would have succeeded, if it hadn't threatened the opium trade of the British. With the help of British and other foreign mercenaries, the Manchus were finally able to defeat the Taipings in 1864, and their Kingdom of Heaven came to an end.

The museum was located in the former residence of Yang Hsiu-ch'ing, the commander-in-chief of Taiping forces. It also included his gardens and even a teahouse. If we had more than a day to spend in Nanking, we would have stayed longer. But we didn't have more than a day, and there was more to see. On our way out, I bought a souvenir. It was an imprint of the seal affixed to all the Taiping decrees issued by the King of

Heaven, as Hung styled himself. I thought maybe I would give it to one of my Christian friends and tell them it was from Jesus Christ's brother, and watch their reaction.

By the time we left, the day was half over, and we were just getting started. Since we were pressed for time, we took another taxi. Our next destination was a kilometer or two to the west. It was the Memorial Hall of the Nanking Massacre. We had already visited the memorial hall at Yuhuatai that commemorated the execution of 100,000 citizens of Nanking by the Nationalists. This one recounted in unforgettable detail an even greater atrocity. When the Japanese captured Nanking in 1937, they massacred over 300,000 people, including women and children. One of the exhibits included a series of articles printed in Japanese newspapers about a contest between two Japanese lieutenants to see who could kill one hundred Chinese fastest, using only their swords.

Reading about these acts and seeing the actual photographs taken by Japanese soldiers left us feeling numb. It's always hard to understand why human beings are capable of such indifference to the suffering of their own kind. The Nanking Massacre, though, was not simply indifference. It was the glorification of murder. When we thought about all the people massacred in Nanking in the 1930s and 1940s by the Japanese and also by their fellow Chinese, we had to wonder why anyone wanted to live here. I suppose because that was where the jobs were. It was the capital.

Nowadays, Nanking is the capital of Kiangsu province. But in the past, it was the capital of a number of dynasties based south of the Yangtze. One such dynasty was the Ming (1368–1644), and its founder also chose Nanking as his capital. It was Nanking's most glorious era. Although there wasn't much left of the Ming in the city, the tomb of its founder, Emperor Hung-wu, was nearby and was our next destination.

Once again, we flagged down a taxi. We didn't have time for buses. We crossed the city from west to east and came out at the base of Tzuchinshan. *Tzu-chin* was a Buddhist term meaning "purple gold," and referred to a type of gold that had a purplish hue. Of the four types Indian Buddhists distinguished, purple gold was considered the best because it most closely resembled the hue of Shakyamuni Buddha's skin.

Sun Yat-sen Mausoleum

From the base of the mountain, we followed a road halfway up to a large parking lot. We told our driver to wait for us, then we paid the admission fee and walked down a long cement path toward Emperor Hung-wu's grave. The path was another spirit way. But it was far more imperial than the one leading to the tomb of the King of Borneo. The statues were huge, averaging about ten feet high. Once again, they included elephants and camels and mythical beasts as well as officials and generals. When we finally reached the tomb, there was a herd of deer grazing on the grass. They didn't seem to mind us and kept on grazing as we walked around the mound.

Although the first Ming emperor was buried here in Nanking, the second Ming emperor moved the capital to Beijing, and all subsequent emperors were buried near the Great Wall. This was Tzuchinshan's sole imperial tomb. But it wasn't its only tomb. We returned to our taxi and headed farther up the mountain to the tomb of Sun Yat-sen.

Sun was born in South China near Kuangchou and was given the name Chung-shan, or Middle Mountain. Sun, though, preferred his sobriquet, which was pronounced *Yi-hsien* in Mandarin and *Yat-sen* in his native Cantonese dialect. Either way, it meant Reclusive Immortal. I don't know about the "reclusive" part, but in death, he certainly had joined their ranks in the minds of his fellow Chinese.

Although Sun died in Beijing in 1925, before he died he asked to be buried in Nanking, and his body was brought here for entombment two years later. Tombs, of course, are for the living and not for the dead, and his countrymen honored his memory with something even grander than the tomb they built for Emperor Hung-wu. After all, Sun also founded a dynasty of sorts, namely the Republican dynasty. Once again, we asked our driver to wait while we paid the admission fee and walked through the gate.

It was suitably massive and at the same time austere. All the building materials were either white or blue, the colors of the Nationalist Party, of which Sun Yat-sen was the founder and leader. It looked like a combination of the Washington Monument and the Lincoln Memorial and consisted of a long series of wide steps divided by a series of archways that ended at a huge mausoleum. The whole place was surrounded by dense groves of dark green pine trees. It was very imposing, and was the one place everyone who came to Nanking tried to visit. Even though it was a weekday, there was a long line of people filing through the mausoleum to view Sun's casket. We joined them and filed past Sun's seated statue, which was carved by the French sculptor Paul Landowski. Then we entered the inner chamber behind the statue and filed past Sun's casket. Unlike Mao's body in Beijing, which floated in a formaldehyde solution inside a crystal casket, Sun's remains were not on display. On top of his casket, though, was a reclining marble likeness.

When I was living in Taiwan, I heard the reason the body wasn't on display was because it was taken to Taiwan by Chiang Kai-shek when he fled there in 1949. But I also heard that the body was returned after his son, Chiang Ching-kuo, became president. Naturally, this wasn't something people liked to talk about. Another indication that the body had, in fact, been returned was that a few months before we visited, a friend of mine accompanied Sun Yat-sen's granddaughter here. Her name was

Nanking's Yangtze River Bridge

Underneath Nanking's Yangtze River Bridge

Nora Sun, and until recently she represented the commercial interests of the U.S. government in China. Strangely (or perhaps not so strangely), it was her first visit to her grandfather's tomb. To avoid making a scene, she decided not to notify the authorities she was coming and filed past her grandfather's casket along with everyone else, just as we did. The line moved fairly quickly. Fifteen minutes after we entered the mausoleum, we were back outside.

After we returned to our taxi, we told the driver we had one more place to visit. We wanted to end our day at the Yangtze River Bridge, which was located at the northwest corner of the city. We crossed the city yet again. But this time, when our driver dropped us off at the base of the bridge, we told him not to wait.

When it was first completed in 1968, the bridge was hailed as a symbol of socialist progress. Its completion, in fact, surprised many people, especially the Russians. The Russians designed the bridge. But in 1960, when relations between the two countries turned sour, the Russian engineers packed up and took their plans home. The Chinese were left with a few cement caissons and no plans. It took them eight more years, but they finally succeeded in forging one of China's most important transportation links. Until it was built, there was no direct rail link between Beijing and Shanghai. The Yangtze River Bridge became a symbol of progress under the banner of Maoist thought, as it was completed during the Cultural Revolution.

It was impressive standing beneath its huge cement arches. We stood there watching trains and cars passing above and ships passing below. At some point, we jumped over the cement retaining wall at the base of the bridge and walked out onto the mud flats along the river for a closer look. A naval patrol boat soon chased us back. We returned to the base of the bridge and took an elevator to the roadway above. We thought we would walk across to Pukou on the other side of the Yangtze. It was only a kilometer away. But we didn't get even halfway. The exhaust fumes were overpowering. We had to give up and head back to the city, back to our hotel, back to an early end to yet another big day.

仙人 茶壺

14. Immortals & Teapots

Well, it was supposed to be an early end to another big day. But it wasn't. We started drinking wine with dinner and continued in our room until midnight. We might not have been on vacation, but every once in a while we acted like it. So it was noon the next day when we finally boarded a bus to our next stop. It was a bus bound for Maoshan,

Ghost bus to Maoshan

Maoshan

and it was the eeriest bus ride we ever took. For the past two thousand years, Maoshan has been one of Taoism's major spiritual centers, so we expected the only daily bus to be packed. But for the first and only time on our entire journey, we were the only passengers. We dubbed it "the ghost bus."

From Nanking, we headed east on the highway that led, well, east. It was the same highway traveled by buses bound for Suchou and Hangchou and even Shanghai. Not far from Nanking, we passed several mountains that were being torn down for their cement. Then we began crossing a vast plain. It was the Yangtze Delta Floodplain. The ocean was less than a hundred kilometers away, but we weren't going that far. Two hours after leaving Nanking, the ghost bus turned off the highway at the village of Tienwangchen, drove north ten kilometers, and dropped us off at the base of Maoshan. It wasn't much of a mountain. But it was the only one around, which made it look bigger. Taoists call it the eastern end of the Kunlun Range that begins in Afghanistan. The reason Taoists went to the trouble of ennobling its slopes and its summit

Maoshan's Chiuhsiao Wanfu Temple

with temples and shrines was because this was where the three Mao brothers came over 2,000 years ago.

They were grandsons of the Taoist master, Mao Meng, who cultivated Taoist yoga and alchemy on Huashan, where he was said to have ascended to Heaven in broad daylight on the back of a dragon. That was around 200 BC. Later, his grandsons took up their grandfather's practice and traveled all the way to this mountain. No one knows why, but they chose its slopes and its summit for their new home, and they never left. Undoubtedly, it had something to do with its geomantic position. It was, after all, the only mountain around. Perhaps the Yangtze had turned it into an island at the time. Perhaps it shimmered in the distance as they approached it, as if it were one of the islands of the immortals. In the centuries that followed, many other Taoists came here to cultivate the way of long life, including T'ao Hung-ching, who completed the first compilation of the Taoist canon during his stay on the mountain in the sixth century. The canon T'ao compiled gave a prominent place to the works of the Mao brothers and their successors, and Maoshan has been a place of pilgrimage ever since—at least until recently.

Despite the mountain's former glory, the stream of pilgrims apparently ended with the Cultural Revolution. Business was so bad, both drivers of the two motorized rickshaws that waited for pilgrims at the base of the mountain were asleep. We left them to their dreams and began hiking up the road that led to the summit. It was five kilometers to the top, and we soon realized we had bitten off more than we could chew. The pilgrim business at Maoshan was so bad there was no place to leave our bags, so we had to carry them. After about a kilometer, we saw a trail on the left that led to a small temple. We thought maybe we could leave our bags there, assuming someone was home. But just then a truck came along, and we waved. The driver stopped and told us to get in the back. A few minutes later we were at the summit, where the Mao brothers turned into cranes and flew off to Heaven over 2,000 years ago.

At 372 meters, Maoshan wasn't an especially high mountain. But the view from the summit was impressive. Below us in all directions stretched a vast plain of rice fields and fishponds. The Taoists who lived here must have felt as if they were just a step away from Heaven, and maybe they were. It would have been a great place to meditate and practice ch'i-kung, or inner alchemy, and for the past 2,000 years Maoshan has been home to thousands of Taoists. But times had changed. Its dozens of temples and shrines were reduced to rubble during the Cultural Revolution. All that remained was the small temple near the mountain's base where the graves of the patriarchs were located, and the larger complex at the summit.

From the parking lot, we walked up the steps and entered Chiuhsiao Wanfukung, the Palace of the Ten Thousand Blessings of the Nine Heavens—or Nine Heaven Temple, for short. There were still several shrine halls, and we visited them all. But most of the buildings were still in ruins. While we were walking around, we met a young Taoist priest and he took us to meet the abbot, whose name was Yen Chih-ken. Master Yen invited us to share some tea with him, and we actually had a nice chat. As we were getting ready to leave, he wished us success and wealth.

I thanked him for his good wishes but suggested success and wealth were probably not what Lao-tzu would have wished for. He laughed, then asked us where we planned to spend the night. When we told him we hoped we could spend it on the mountain, he invited us to stay at his temple. The sun looked like it was about two hours from setting, and we were glad to accept. He then asked his attendant to show us to a room, then take us to the guest hall to register. Unfortunately, after we dropped our bags in one of the rooms and went to register, the official assigned by the government to oversee religious affairs at the complex overruled the abbot. He said it would be impossible. He said there weren't any rooms available. This was, of course, ridiculous. We had just put our bags in one of the rooms. It was empty, and so were all the other rooms on that floor. In this case, rolling up my sleeve and showing him my scars would not have helped. This wasn't about whether we were really pilgrims, it was about the nature of Taoism.

Taoism, not Buddhism, is China's national religion. And its national religion has been the source for most of its revolutionary movements over the past two thousand years. Despite the government's overt policy of religious freedom, it is still worried that such freedom might someday bring about its own downfall. Hence, Taoist centers are subject to much tighter control than Buddhist centers. There was nothing we could do. We walked back to the room where we dropped our bags and hoisted them on our backs, then went to say good-bye to the abbot. We thanked him for his offer of hospitality. He sighed, and so did we. He was the abbot, but he was not in charge. We walked back out to the parking lot and began walking down the mountain. The sun was going down, and we had no idea where we were going to spend the night.

At least we didn't have to walk the entire five kilometers. About half-way down, the same truck that picked us up earlier picked us up again. The driver said he brought supplies to the monastery once a day, and he was heading home. His home was in the village at the bottom of the mountain, but he drove a bit past the village and dropped us off at a place where he said the last bus of the day would be passing by. Thirty minutes later, it picked us up. And thirty minutes later, it dropped us off in the village of Tienwangchen, back on the highway that connected Nanking with the cities to the east. Since one of them was our next destination, we felt relieved.

However, by the time we got to the highway, the sun was down, and it was getting dark. Every few minutes a bus came by and we waved, but the drivers didn't slow down. Finally, we came up with a plan. We walked down the road a few hundred meters to the village's one and only stoplight. We figured we had a better chance of flagging down a bus if it had to stop, and the stoplight looked like the right place. Still, over the next hour dozens of buses stopped at the stoplight but ignored us and continued on. Finally, as our faith in the road gods was just about gone, a bus bound for Hangchou picked us up. It was crowded with Uighurs from northwest China on their way to work in that city's textile factories. There weren't any seats, but there was room for us to sit in the stairwell. It wasn't comfortable, but at least we weren't still waving at buses on the highway. Two hours later the driver dropped us off at the edge of Yihsing, which was where we wanted to go. Apparently, the place where the driver dropped us off was where other drivers dropped their passengers off. There were several motorized rickshaws waiting to take people into town. After a brief negotiation, one of them delivered us to the Yihsing Hotel for 10RMB. We were relieved. It wasn't the summit of Maoshan, but we were looking forward to a hot bath and something to eat. Unfortunately, when we went inside, our bad karma was still with us. The desk clerk said the hotel was full. No rooms. When we asked where else we could stay, he said the nearest hotel that accepted foreigners was ten kilometers away in Tingshu. And the last bus to Tingshu, he said, left hours ago.

We could see it was useless to argue with him. We obviously didn't look like the hotel's usual clientele. Naturally, we realized he was just getting rid of us. But it was late, and we were tired, and we really didn't have any other option. So we tried something we had never tried before. We walked over to the far corner of the lobby where there was a set of stairs going up to the second floor, and we did the unthinkable. In the space below the stairs, we put down our bags and took out some clothes, and laid them down on the floor. Then we lay down on top of our clothes and stretched out for the night. The hotel staff was aghast. They obviously hadn't dealt with Hobos from Hell before. When they tried to evict us, we simply curled up and held our ground. This was, we said, the only hotel in town where foreigners were allowed to stay. We had no choice. We couldn't help it if we weren't allowed to stay elsewhere. We suggested they call the police and see if there wasn't an empty jail cell. It was a brazen ploy. But it was like gambling with the house's money. We figured we couldn't lose.

Of course, the reason we dared the hotel staff to call the police was because there was no such thing as a full hotel in China. It was just a question of a person's status in the party or the government or, in our case, a person's persistence. In this case, persistence won out. When other guests began coming over to see what was going on, the staff finally gave up and told us to take our pick of the rooms down an adjoining hallway. It turned out that all the rooms in the hallway were empty, over thirty of them. The next morning, the hall maid told us that the manager liked to save as many rooms as possible, just in case a delegation of visiting officials showed up. Obviously, it was a state-run hotel.

We thanked the maid for the information and went to check out. It had been such a good night—the bath water was hot and the restaurant was still open when we got there, we thanked the desk clerk and told him the room was very nice. And it was—quite a change from the room at Nine Heaven Temple where we had hoped to spend the night. Then we went outside to face the day.

Outside was Yihsing. We had already visited China's porcelain capital. Yihsing was its pottery capital. But when we asked at several nearby stores where we could see how the town's famous pottery was made, we found out that Yihsing was not the place. All the pottery stamped with the name Yihsing on it was produced in the town of Tingshu ten kilometers to the south. It was the old story of the administrative center lending its name to anything produced within its jurisdiction.

Fortunately, buses left for Tingshu every thirty minutes—not at night, but during the day. We stashed our bags at the bus station and caught

Yihsing potter Chang Hsin-lan with author (photo by Steven R. Johnson)

Artisan making teapots in Yihsing

the next one bound for Tingshu. When we boarded, we asked the driver if he knew of a factory there that we could visit. He said we either had to join a tour group or hire a guide at one of the local travel agencies. In Chingtechen we hired a guide, and that worked out fine. So we assumed we would do the same when we got to Tingshu. It turned out we didn't have to. The girl who was sitting in the seat in front of us turned out to be a potter at Tingshu's most famous factory: the Yihsing Purple Clay Artware Factory. Her name was Chang Hsin-lan. When we asked her how long she had been making pottery, she said her father taught her when she was still a child. The road gods had smiled upon us once more. When we told her we were interested in teapots, she said they were what her factory was famous for. After we arrived in Tingshu, she led us there and even introduced us to its deputy director, Li Ch'ang-hung.

Mister Li was also one of the factory's master potters, and he told us everything we wanted to know about the factory and its teapots. Considering our reception at the hotel the previous night, we sensed a change in our karmic winds. Mister Li said the factory was the oldest,

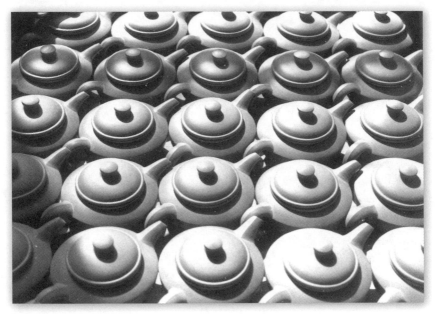

Yihsing teapots

the largest, and the most famous pottery factory in Tingshu. It sounded like a sales pitch, but we didn't care. We were happy, and he wasn't trying to sell us anything. As its name suggested, the factory was famous for its purple clay pottery—which was a very nice shade of brown, as were all the factories in Tingshu.

The clay was the secret to Tingshu's fame. It came from two nearby mountains: Tingshan and Shushan. Mister Li said it took one thousand kilos of unrefined soil from the two mountains to produce one kilo of high-grade clay suitable for teapots or other artware. Once the clay was refined, it was distributed to more than a thousand potters. In the case of teapots, he said each worker made an average of two pots per day. However, the factory's eleven master potters made as few as one per month.

Although Tingshu potters had been making pottery since the Sung dynasty, factory-style production, according to Mister Li, had only been going on since 1956. Since we weren't really interested in factory-style production, we asked if we could see the factory's small-scale production process. He smiled and nodded his head and led us into a

Earthenware pots on a canal barge

series of workrooms where we could see the company's master potters and apprentice potters making teapots. Among the master potters, he introduced us to China's only living national master. His name was Ku Ching-chou. Mister Li said Mister Ku only made four pots per year and that seven years earlier when one of Ku's teapots was put on the market, it sold for 120,000RMB, or $25,000. We stood there in disbelief. Mister Ku just laughed. So did Mister Li.

Altogether, Mister Li spent about an hour leading us around and showing us the production process. He was very generous with his time and showed us everything. What impressed us the most was how well lit the rooms were—with natural light, not overhead lights, and how unhurried the potters were. Once their pots were finished, they were air-dried for several days, depending on the weather, then put in kilns and fired at 1,200 degrees centigrade. Tingshu's purple clay was so oily, it didn't require a glaze, and teapots made with this clay were a joy to hold as well as behold. They felt good in the hand. Wherever Chinese live, they all need a good teapot. And Yihsing teapots are the best. However, fame has a price. Unlike the kaolin clay of Chingtechen, Tingshu's purple clay, according to Mister Li, was not expected to last much longer. He estimated it would be gone within fifty years. It was a sad thought.

With that in mind, we considered buying a few teapots. But when we considered how rough we traveled, we decided they would break and refrained. We thanked Mister Li for taking the time to show us around. We looked for Ms. Chang, but she was already off somewhere working on her next pot. As we walked back out onto the road, we couldn't help noticing that the town was crisscrossed by canals, and the canals were full of barges stacked with huge clay pots and cases packed with tiny teapots. I was looking forward to making tea when I got home. Years earlier, I'd bought a teapot from Yihsing, but now I knew why it made such good tea.

無錫 常熟

15. Wuhsi & Changshu

Having satisfied our curiosity about teapots, we took the next bus back to Yihsing, collected our bags, and boarded a noon bus to Wuhsi. Three thousand years ago, Wuhsi was called Youhsi. *You-hsi* means "lots-of-tin." A thousand years later, the town's tin mines ran out of tin, just as Tingshu was about to run out of purple clay, and the

Fishing boats on Taihu Lake

town's name was changed to Wuhsi, meaning "no-tin." Tin was import-ant because it made bronze possible. No tin, no bronze. And bronze was something anyone rich or powerful had to have. Ritual implements were all made of bronze, and no ceremony could be conducted without it.

From Yihsing, the road to No Tin skirted Lake Taihu. Depending on the season, Taihu was China's third or fourth largest freshwater lake, and it supplied most of the water for the canal system that crisscrossed the intersection of Kiangsu and Chekiang provinces. It was also home to thirty varieties of fish, and one of the most beautiful sights in that part of China were the sails of its fishing fleet, which numbered in the hundreds.

As our bus bumped along, we gazed at the lake and the sails and tried to imagine all the rocks just below the surface. In addition to its fish and its fishing boats, the lake was famous for its rocks. The rocks were brought here from different parts of China and placed beneath the water line, then left here for years, until they had been weathered by the action of the waves and the tides. The weathering transformed the rocks into the strangest of shapes, and they have become a mainstay of any traditional Chinese garden. We thought we might see signs of them. But we didn't see even a ripple.

By the time we reached Wuhsi, it was one o'clock. No doubt Wuhsi had sights worth seeing, but we had come here to see something else, something outside Wuhsi. We stashed our bags at the bus station and asked directions to the village of Machen. Thirty minutes later, we were on a local bus headed in that direction. And thirty minutes after that, we were there. Earlier, we had worried we might not arrive in time. But it was only two o'clock. We had plenty of time. The reason for our coun-tryside excursion was that Machen was the hometown of one of China's two greatest travelers, and we wanted to pay our respects. The traveler's name was Hsu Hsia-k'o, and he was born here in 1587.

Unlike the seventh-century monk Hsuan-tsang, who traveled all the way to India and back, Hsu Hsia-k'o did all his traveling inside China. And unlike Hsuan-tsang, who traveled for the sake of the Dharma, Hsu traveled for the sake of mountains. During the course of twenty-six years, he visited every important mountain in China. But he didn't just

霞客先生遺像

Portrait of Hsu Hsia-k'o

travel, he wrote about his travels. And he wrote a lot. Although much of his travel writing was lost, his surviving diaries still contain over 400,000 characters. The diaries that did survive have become the standard by which China's scenic wonders are still described. People still use his words to describe a waterfall or a rock pinnacle. He immortalized China's natural world.

When Hsu wasn't traveling, he lived at his family home in the tiny village of Machen. The village wasn't much more than a wide place in the road. But there were several stores that sold things like farm equipment and household necessities. We went into one and asked directions. The owner pointed us down a dirt road that led away from the highway and into the countryside. We walked about 300 meters and approached the front gate of a building. A sign said this was the Hsu Hsia-k'o Memorial Hall.

As we walked through the gate and entered the hall, we discovered the depth of our karmic connection with China's greatest travel writer. The only person there besides ourselves was the director, Liu Cheng-ch'uan. Mister Liu was so surprised to see us, he walked over and started shaking our hands, and he kept shaking our hands, as if we were old friends. The memorial hall didn't get many visitors, so we thought that was the reason for Mister Liu's warm reception. Or maybe, we thought, it was because we were foreigners. But that wasn't it either.

Once he stopped shaking our hands, Mister Liu led us into his office. Then he opened a drawer in his desk and took out several envelopes. They were all stamped. We shrugged. What was this all about? Liu waved them in our faces and said he had just picked them up at the post office. They were first-day-of-issue commemorative envelopes. We looked at the stamp. It showed a picture of Hsu Hsia-k'o wearing his travel clothes and making notes in his travel diary. Then we looked at the postmark. It was dated October 18, 1991. Then we looked at the calendar on the wall in Mister Liu's office. We were there on October 19, 1991. Then we looked at the envelope again. In addition to a stamp of Hsu Hsia-k'o, there was a photograph of his grave. It turned out 1991 was the 350th anniversary of his death. "*Omitofo*," we all said in unison.

Mister Liu said he would be honored if we would accept the envelopes, and he wrote our names on them in the space for addressees. It was like receiving a personal letter from Hsu Hsia-k'o: "Hope you're well, Bill. You wouldn't believe how beautiful it is here at the summit of Huangshan. Hope you can come yourself someday. But don't tell anyone. I would hate to see this mountain overrun." A finer gift would be hard to imagine for travelers like ourselves. Meanwhile, I reached into my bag and showed Mister Liu my copies of Hsu's travel diaries. We relied on them when we visited Hengshan and Lushan and Huangshan. The temples and pavilions had changed, but the paths were still the same.

After we recovered from the surprise of such serendipity, we put the commemorative envelopes in our bags, and Mister Liu showed us around the memorial hall. It included maps of Hsu's journeys and photographs of the mountains he visited taken by modern travelers. And, of course, there were excerpts from his travel diaries. There wasn't a lot to see, but we were easily satisfied. It was a special day, and we were there, and that was good enough.

Mister Liu then escorted us back outside and a hundred meters down the road to another hall. The second hall was filled with Hsu's own calligraphy along with that of his ancestors and his descendants. Although he wasn't wealthy, Hsu represented the 17th generation of an illustrious family, a family that was still flourishing. Mister Liu said members of the family's 26th and 27th generations still lived in the area. There was also a portrait of Hsu based on an inscription that described him as "dark-skinned, buck-toothed and six-feet tall"—the very image of an ancient man of the Way.

Hsu was born here in 1586 and died here in 1641, 350 years and a day before our visit. The cause of his death was lacquer poisoning, which he contracted during his travels in the jungles of southwest China. Once, when I was hiking in the Chungnan Mountains south of Sian, I saw a man suffering from lacquer poisoning. His head was swollen to twice its normal size. Simply coming into contact with the sap of the lacquer tree was enough.

Mister Liu then led us outside to a garden courtyard at the far end of which was Hsu's grave. We didn't have any whiskey with us or we

Hsu Hsia-k'o's grave

would have offered him some. Instead, we bowed in front of his grave and thanked him for showing us the path. We often felt as if we were following in his footsteps. Before we left, Mister Liu pointed to several dead trees in the courtyard and the faint line of mud halfway up Hsu's tombstone. He said it was the high-water line from a recent flood that had inundated the area a few months earlier. The Yangtze was less than twenty kilometers to the north, and this was, after all, the Yangtze Delta Floodplain.

It was with reluctance that we finally said good-bye to Mister Liu and thanked him for the first-day-of-issue envelopes. I still have mine at home. I use it as a bookmark in my copy of *Hsu Hsia-k'o's Travel Diaries*. Every time I open the book, I think of Mister Liu and hope he's well.

By the time we returned to Wuhsi, the sun was thinking of going down. We reclaimed our bags at the bus station and looked for a hotel to spend the night. We didn't see anything near the bus station and asked a taxi driver to take us to a hotel by the lake. Why not, we thought, spend the night next to Taihu? The driver delivered us to the Hupin Hotel. It was a really nice hotel and in a beautiful setting, right on the shore of

Early morning Changshu skyline

Lake Taihu. We weren't sure we could afford it, but a room with three beds was only 130RMB. Unlike the previous night, we didn't have to stretch out below the stairs. They had plenty of rooms. Ours even had a view of the lake. We also dined in the hotel restaurant for a change. It was just as good as the dinner we had at the Maple Hotel in Changsha. Among the dishes we had that were sufficiently memorable to note in our journals were several for which the city was rightfully famous: fried gluten, Wuhsi-style pork ribs, and deep-fried white bait.

After dinner, we walked out to the lakeshore. The hotel was located on an arm of the lake that formed Wuhsi's harbor. Even though the sun was down, there were still a few boats coming back after a day of fishing or rock harvesting. In the distance, we could see the small rise of Turtlehead Island. There was a pier in front of the hotel where boats departed for tours of the lake. But it was too late for a tour, and we just sat down on the hotel's grass lawn and enjoyed the view. We were living large again. Unfortunately, we weren't really vacationing, and one night was all we stayed.

The next morning, we bid farewell to the town with no tin and caught an early morning bus to Changshu. It was only forty-four kilometers to the east, and we were there before nine. After depositing our bags at the bus station as usual, we took two rickshaws to see a few sights—the three of us couldn't fit in one. Changshu wasn't a major tourist destination, and rickshaws were still the major form of public transportation in the city, other than buses, of course.

Our destination was a mountain on the western edge of the city. It was called Yushan. It wasn't a big mountain, but we weren't really interested in the mountain. We asked our rickshaw drivers to take us to the mountain's southeast corner. We thought we would begin the day by visiting the graves of the city's two most famous residents.

The first belonged to Yen Tzu-you, and it was right next to the road. Yen Tzu-you was born in Changshu, but he left when he was young to study with Confucius. He ended up becoming one of Confucius's favorite students and was, in fact, the only southerner among the Master's inner circle. When later Confucians developed their pantheon of heroes, he was numbered among the Master's ten most prominent disciples. After Confucius died, Master Yen, as he became known, returned to Changshu and was instrumental in spreading his master's teachings in this part of China. He was buried here in 443 BC. Most people don't realize that while the history of China goes back 5,000 years, Chinese culture didn't reach this region until the first millennium BC. And it was people like Master Yen who brought it here.

After paying our respects at Master Yen's grave, we followed the trail behind it that led up the mountain and through a series of stone arches. Two hundred meters later, we reached the grave of Chung Yung. Chung Yung was the second son of the ruler of the state of Chou, which was centered around the modern city of Sian. When the king decided to bypass his two older sons and turn over his throne to his youngest son's son, Chung Yung and his elder brother took this as a sign of their father's displeasure and left. And they didn't just move to the suburbs. It was as if they were exiled. While Chung Yung's nephew went on to found the Chou dynasty, Chung Yung led a thousand of his retainers over a thousand kilometers to the Yangtze Delta and settled near Changshu.

Archway leading to grave of Confucius's disciple

This was around 1100 BC, when the Yangtze Delta was inhabited by ethnic groups other than Han Chinese. Chung Yung and his followers introduced Han culture to the region, and the region has been a center of Han culture ever since. Along with writing and technical skills, Chung Yung also introduced agriculture, and the region became one of the wealthiest areas in ancient China. When he died, Chung Yung was buried on Yushan. In fact, the mountain's name came from the first part of another name by which he was known, Yu-chung.

In addition to its two famous graves, the mountain was dotted with terraces and pavilions, and groups of old men were sitting beneath the pavilions drinking tea or practicing their ch'i-kung exercises on the terraces—the two favorite morning rituals of old men in China. After wandering around the mountain for a while, we walked back down to Master Yen's grave and hired another pair of rickshaws to take us farther along the road skirting the eastern flank of the mountain.

At one point, the driver whose rickshaw was carrying me and Finn began panting so heavily, we thought he was going to have a heart attack. We got out and started walking, but he insisted we climb back in. Somehow he managed to pedal us to our final destination: Hsingfu Temple. We thanked him for his effort and paid him three times what he asked, which was 10RMB instead of 3RMB.

Hsingfu Temple had been one of the most famous Buddhist temples south of the Yangtze, ever since it was built 1,400 years ago. Although it had been home to many famous monks, it was no longer a monastery. Like many monasteries, it was now administered as a tourist site by the officials in charge of cultural affairs. On the side road leading to its front gate, we passed a cemetery containing the graves of some of its famous monks of the past. At least the man in charge of the temple said they were famous. I didn't recognize any of their names. Their nicknames, though, were colorful enough: Yen-ch'eng, "subduer of tigers"; Ch'ang-ta, "conqueror of dragons"; Huai-shu, "the patched robe monk who faces the sun"; and Wu-en, "reader of sutras in the moonlight." But no one at the temple had ever heard of the monk who led us here.

He was born in Changshu in 1272, and he lived at Hsingfu Temple when he first became a monk. His Buddhist name was Ch'ing-kung, but he was better known as Shih-wu, or Stonehouse, after a cave not far from the temple where he used to meditate. Eventually Stonehouse moved to a mountain south of Lake Taihu and spent most of his remaining years in a hut at its summit. He also wrote poems, and he wrote this preface for them:

> *Here in the woods I have lots of time. When I don't spend it sleeping, I enjoy composing poems. But with paper and ink so scarce, I haven't written them down. Now some Zen monks have asked me to record what I find of interest on this mountain. I've sat here quietly and let my brush fly. Suddenly this volume is full. I close it and send it back down with the admonition not to try singing these poems. Only if you sit on them will they do you any good.*

The reason we were looking for him was that a number of years ago, I published English translations of his *Mountain Poems*, like this one, #36:

> *I was a Zen monk who didn't know Zen*
> *so I chose the woods for the years I had left*
> *a robe made of patches over my body*
> *a belt of bamboo around my waist*
> *mountains and streams explain Bodhidharma's meaning*
> *flower smiles and bird songs reveal the hidden key*
> *sometimes I sit on a flat-topped rock*
> *late cloudless nights once a month*

Even if it wasn't nighttime, that seemed like a good idea. We walked out of the monastery and found an unoccupied pavilion. It wasn't a flat-topped rock, but it looked like a good place to sit down. And so we did. We spent the rest of the morning just sitting there listening to the birds and enjoying the flower-scented mountain air. This was some kind of vacation.

蘇州

16. Suchou

Our next stop was Suchou, surely one of the finest places in China to spend a few days, if not weeks. From Changshu, it only took a little over an hour to get there by bus. It wasn't even noon when we checked into the cheap wing of the Nanlin Hotel, where a room with three beds went for 60RMB, or $12. For Suchou, that was a great deal.

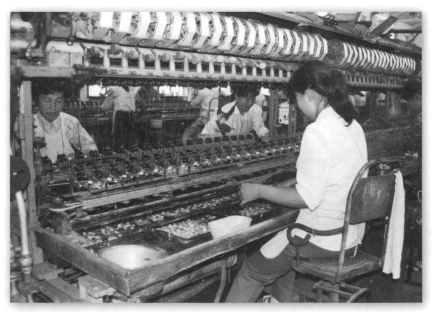

Suchou silk factory

Most of the other hotels for foreigners were in the same area, and their prices were also for foreigners.

Since it was still too early to put an end to the day, we strolled down the street. We didn't go far. Suchou is famous for its gardens, and one of the nicest was a few short blocks from our hotel. It was first laid out in the twelfth century then abandoned for 600 years. When it was restored in the eighteenth century, people referred to it as Wangssu Garden after the name of a nearby alley. But at some point someone changed the name to Wangshih Garden, or Master of Nets Garden. The pronunciation in the Suchou dialect was the same, but the fishing image was more poetic than the alley's name, and it fit with the garden's original name, which was Yuyin (Fisherman Recluse) Garden. At least, that was the story the woman who guided us through the garden told us.

It was the smallest public garden in Suchou, but it was one of the city's best. Despite its relatively small size at just over an acre, the views created by the designer were constantly changing. Every few feet there was another delightful combination of water and plants and rocks and architecture. We could have spent the rest of the day there, but we decided to go back to our hotel, take a nap, and return after dinner. At night the garden looked just as lovely, but there were musicians. Each of the garden's pavilions featured someone playing a different classical instrument or singing a different song form. Not many people realize that Suchou is just as famous for its traditional music as it is for its gardens. We stayed until the garden closed at nine o'clock, but we weren't done for the night. There was a moon outside, and our hotel had a small hill. We bought a few bottles of beer and watched the late-night performance of the moon and the clouds.

The next morning we left to see a few more sights, but we didn't get far before we discovered that Suchou was a different kind of Chinese city. There was a bakery just outside the hotel front gate, and it sold croissants—fresh croissants, baked that morning. We had never had a croissant in China, not even a stale one, much less a fresh one. But Suchou was that kind of city. For all its traditional culture, it was cosmopolitan. And so we ventured into the day with croissants in hand

and a plan. We decided to visit the western part of town and to go there by boat. The Chinese like to call Suchou the Venice of Asia, and it has enough canals and bridges crisscrossing the city to merit the title, thirty-five kilometers of canals and 168 bridges. We told a boat-man waiting for fares in a nearby canal to take us to Liuyuan Garden. Thirty minutes later, we were there. Of course, there are better gardens in Suchou, but they are all on the tour group itinerary, and we like to avoid crowds. So we opted for two of the less visited and were glad we did.

The name of the garden was apt. In Chinese it means "Stay a While." And we did. It was the opposite of the Master of the Nets Garden we visited the day before. At seven and a half acres, it's the biggest garden in Suchou. Hence, the designer didn't feel compelled to change a visitor's view every few feet. He took his time, and so did we. We were actually able to walk around alone and not in a crowd. It was a simple garden but also not a simple garden. We especially enjoyed the different-shaped windows along the walkways that circled the ponds. They reminded us how our view of something is shaped by how it is framed.

After we had stayed a while and done enough strolling, we continued on to another garden a hundred meters farther down the canal. It was called West Garden Temple, after the temple it was a part of. Although the two gardens were designed 400 years ago by the same man, West Temple Garden was unique in its open, almost park-like atmosphere. There were even grassy areas where a visitor could sit down and watch the clouds overhead. In fact, that was the difference between the two gardens. In the first one, we strolled. In the second one, we sat.

But being travelers, even in such a restful place, we didn't sit long. We went back outside and flagged down another canal taxi. We told the boatman to take us to Hanshan Temple. The tourist brochures all said the temple was named after the Buddhist poet who lived there in the T'ang dynasty before he went off to become a hermit near Tientai. But Han-shan, or Cold Mountain, as he is known in the West, never lived there. The temple was named for a nearby hill.

Suchou canal

Suchou's Liuyuan Garden

I'm guessing there aren't many Chinese who don't know the poem by Chang Chi titled "Anchored Overnight at Maple Bridge":

Crows caw the moon sets frost fills the sky
river maples fishing fires care-plagued sleep
coming from Cold Mountain Temple outside the Suchou wall
the sound of the midnight bell reaches a traveler's boat

It's one of the most famous poems in the Chinese language. But Chang Chi wrote that poem in 742, when Han-shan would have been less than ten. And yet, the myth of the temple's association with the hermit has survived.

The reason we wanted to go there was to meet the temple's abbot. Eight years earlier, I published a translation of Cold Mountain's 300-odd poems, and a friend showed the abbot a copy of my book. Ever since then, the abbot and I had been corresponding. His name was Hsing-k'ung, and he was also an artist. He sent me paintings and calligraphy, and I sent him copies of my books. But I hadn't heard from him for several years, and I wasn't sure if he was still alive.

We inquired at the gate, and one of the monks ushered us into the abbot's reception room. It looked more like an art studio. All the walls were covered with paintings and calligraphy, and half the room was taken up by a large table covered with sheets of *hsuan-chih* waiting for inspiration. As we entered, we saw Hsing-k'ung sitting down talking to another monk. He looked up and smiled, and we walked over and introduced ourselves. I started to tell him that I had looked forward to meeting him for many years. But I didn't get that far. He jumped up and grabbed my hand, and never let go. I mean, for the next hour he never let go. We talked and talked, and he never let go. Finally, he got up to show us around the temple and finally let go of my hand. But then he grabbed my arm.

What he wanted to show us was the temple's calligraphy, which included a wall on which was written the entire *Diamond Sutra*. It was done by one of the most famous calligraphers of the Sung dynasty,

Master Hsing-k'ung with author (photo by Steven R. Johnson)

Chang Chi-chih (aka Shu-liao), and it included a colophon by Tung Ch'i-ch'ang, one of the most famous calligraphers of the Ming. The wall was a national treasure. Hsing-k'ung also showed us the temple's famous Ming dynasty portraits of Cold Mountain and his friend Pickup. Although neither man ever lived at the temple, they had become inseparable from the temple in people's imaginations. Of course, we said nothing to dissuade the abbot of such a view.

Hsing-k'ung also showed us where he planned to build a new pagoda. It was going to be huge, and we wondered where the money was going to come from. Clearly, the temple was doing well. Maybe it would be coming from the abbot's paintings and calligraphy, both of which, I heard, sold for small fortunes in Japan. After showing us around, Hsing-k'ung led us back to his reception room, and he gave each of us one of his paintings. The one he gave me was of an iris and still hangs on my wall at home. Finally, we got up to leave, and I promised to send him a copy of my next book, and he finally let go of my arm.

Suchou is one of those towns where visitors never have enough time.

A week would have been about right. But, as usual, we only had a day. As we came out of the temple, we flagged down a taxi and headed back to our hotel. Instead of more gardens and temples, we wanted to find out about silk. Silk was the miracle fiber that made the city's gardens and temples possible. Money from the silk trade financed everything.

Archaeologists had found signs of early silk production near the middle reaches of the Yellow River and also in the lower reaches of the Yangtze, not far from Suchou. The materials they found dated back nearly 5,000 years. Ironically, that was the same period when Lei Tsu was said to have invented silk. Like all proper inventions, it happened by chance. Lei Tsu was drinking tea under a mulberry tree when a silkworm cocoon fell from the tree into her cup. When she tried to extract the cocoon from her tea, she caught hold of the filament and began unreeling. And so silk was discovered while Lei Tsu was drinking tea. Lei Tsu, incidentally, was the wife of the Yellow Emperor, who ruled the middle reaches of the Yellow River between 2,700 and 2,600 BC, or nearly 5,000 years ago.

Although the manufacture of silk apparently began at several places in China around that time, for the past thousand years its main center was the Suchou area. This was because silkworms only ate mulberry leaves, and mulberry trees seemed to do best around Suchou. Then, too, Suchou's location on the Grand Canal and also near the mouth of the Yangtze guaranteed it easy access to markets, both domestic and foreign.

After stopping at our hotel long enough to drop off our newly acquired paintings, we headed for Suchou's Number-One Silk Mill. It was a twenty-minute walk south of our hotel, beyond the city's ancient moat. The previous afternoon, we asked our hotel to call ahead, so we were expected. A woman in charge of receiving guests led us into a room, served us some tea, and told us about the silkworm. She said each silk moth lays about 400 eggs, and as soon as the eggs hatch, the new silkworms begin eating mulberry leaves. Over the course of twenty-five days, each worm eats about twenty-five grams of leaves. As it does, it goes through five stages of development. Finally, after the fifth stage, it stops eating and begins spinning a cocoon around itself. The cocoon only takes twenty-four hours to spin, and it consists of 1,200 meters of filament—which the silkworm makes by digesting mulberry leaves. The woman who explained this process to us said that if the silkworms were left alone, they would emerge seven days later as silk moths. But if they did, they would break the filament, making the cocoons useless for silk production. To prevent this from happening, 85 percent of the cocoons are immersed in boiling water for fifteen minutes, while the remaining 15 percent are set aside for reproduction.

Once we finished our tea, our guide led us into the factory where we watched women workers sorting the boiled cocoons. After sorting, the cocoons are unreeled not just one at a time, but nine at a time. Our guide said that it takes nine filaments to form a single silk thread, a thread that is strong enough to weave and is 1,200 meters long. Nothing, she said, is wasted. Once the silk filaments are unreeled, the dead pupas inside the cocoons are set aside for use in a medicine for diabetes. Meanwhile, the resulting thread is immersed in hot wax for twenty minutes to soften the fiber and to prepare it for dying. Then it is woven into bolts and sent to other factories for dying and printing, and finally to yet more factories for cutting and sewing into garments. She said that it takes 900 cocoons to produce enough thread to make a silk skirt or shirt. A silk tie, she said, requires 120.

It was at this point that our guide finally led us into the factory showroom and said good-bye. The showroom was full of dresses and shirts and, of course, bolts of silk. It was all very fine and colorful, but we didn't really want to buy anything. It had been a fairly full day, and we suddenly realized we were hungry.

Suchou was full of fine restaurants, and people came from as far away as Shanghai and Nanking to have dinner here. In fall, they come for Suchou's freshwater crabs, steamed and eaten with soy sauce and ginger. And, of course, we were there in fall. With this in mind, we walked back across the moat and past our hotel all the way to Kuanchien Street, where many of the city's finer restaurants were located. We thought about eating at the famous Sungholou Restaurant. But it looked too fancy for us. We were looking for something simpler. While we were walking around trying to decide where and what to eat, we saw a line trailing out the front door of a restaurant in Tachien Alley. That's always a good sign. So we got in line. The name of the place was the Green Willow Wonton Shop. Even with the long line, it only took us fifteen minutes to work our way to the front and place our order. At least we didn't have to worry about what to order. They only made two things: wonton soup and shrimp-and-pork dumplings. It wasn't crab, but it was delicious. For the past thousand years, the Chinese have said people who live in Suchou are lucky. We had to agree.

隱者 真珠

17. Hermits & Pearls

It was hard to leave Suchou. On our way out of the Nanlin the next morning, we bought enough freshly-baked croissants to get us through the day. Finding a croissant in China was such a treat. But by the time we reached the long-distance bus station at the north end of town, they were gone. *C'est la vie.* An hour later, we were on a bus bound for Huchou and our last province. Good-bye Kiangsu, hello Chekiang.

Location of Stonehouse's old hut

Huchou means "lake town," the lake being, of course, Taihu. We were circumambulating it. We had already visited Yihsing on its west shore and Wuhsi on its north shore and Suchou on its east shore. Huchou was on its south shore. Huchou didn't attract many tourists, but we weren't going there to see anything in Huchou. We wanted to visit the mountain where Stonehouse lived. We had already visited the monastery in Changshu where he became a monk back when Kublai Khan ruled China from his pleasure dome. We didn't expect to find Stonehouse's hut, but we hoped at least to find his mountain.

We had visited similar sights that weren't on the tourist circuit but that appealed to our peculiar tastes, like the graves of Tu Fu, T'ao Yuan-ming, and Ch'u Yuan. Stonehouse, or Shih-wu as he was known, was in a different class. He was hardly known outside the small circle of Buddhists who had read his poems. It was a small circle and likely to remain so. Even the people in his hometown had never heard of him. We didn't know much more than they did, except that Stonehouse built his hut just below the summit of a mountain called Hsiamushan, which was somewhere south of Huchou. Unfortunately, I was unable to find a map with the mountain's name on it. So we were going there blind. But lately the road gods had smiled upon us, and we thought perhaps they would smile upon us once more.

Two hours after leaving Suchou, our bus pulled into Lake City. We got out and went inside the bus station, and looked at the route map on the bus station wall. We picked a town about thirty kilometers to the south called Teching. We reasoned that Hsiamushan must be one of the mountains west of Teching. We figured if we hiked into the mountains, we might get lucky and find it. So I walked over to the ticket window and asked for three tickets on the next bus.

As I said, not many tourists, much less foreigners, passed through Huchou. When the ticket seller saw us, she left and returned a few minutes later with the station's party secretary. He asked us where we wanted to go, and I repeated what I told the woman. He sold us the tickets, but he suggested we would be more comfortable waiting for the bus in his office. A crowd of on-lookers had already begun to form around us, and the bus wasn't due to leave for another hour. Naturally, we were happy to accept his offer.

As he led us into his office, he introduced himself. His name was Kao Yung-k'uei. When he asked us why we wanted to go to Teching, we told him we were looking for a mountain west of Teching where a poet lived in the fourteenth century. We asked him if he had heard of Hsiamushan. He shook his head. Then he told us to sit down on the sofa, while he left to get some glasses for tea. While he was gone, I gazed around his office. What was that? Right behind where we were sitting was a detailed topographic map of the county. I was amazed and started poring over the area south of Huchou. Thirty seconds later, my eyes came to rest on, you guessed it, Hsiamushan. Eureka, it actually existed! And after 600 years, the name was still the same.

When Mister Kao returned, we told him to forget about the bus to Teching, we wanted to go to Hsiamushan. He was a true bodhisattva sent down to help others. He not only refunded our tickets, he went outside the station and arranged for a taxi to take us to Hsiamushan. While we were waiting, I continued to pore over the map. Eureka again. Just south of town was Taochangshan. Taochangshan was another mountain where Stonehouse once lived. And the temple where he lived was still there—at least the name was on the map. We couldn't believe our good fortune. It was one thing to follow the tourist brochures and guidebooks. It was quite another to discover something of interest that no one had ever written about and to which no signs pointed. We were in traveler heaven. A minute later, Mister Kao returned and led us outside and introduced us to our driver. We told Mister Kao we wanted to go to Taochangshan then Hsiamushan, and he conveyed this to the driver. The driver shrugged and said the fee for both places would be the same, 50RMB. It was such a small price to pay, we gladly agreed. We stashed our bags at the station luggage depository and waved good-bye to Mister Kao.

About two kilometers south of town, we turned off the main road then drove as far as we could on a dirt road. When the road finally ended, we walked up a trail to what was left of Wanshou Temple. A thousand years ago, it was one of the ten most famous Zen centers in

Sung dynasty pagoda on Taochangshan

China, and it was where Stonehouse lived with his master before moving to Hsiamushan. It was also where he later gave sermons on the rare occasions when he came down the mountain.

Inside the main hall, we met the abbot. His name was Fu-hsing. I had to ask him to write down the characters. They were so unusual. I had never heard them, much less seen them. Together they meant "fragrant fragrance." It was a Buddhist name, a very unique Buddhist name. He said the Red Guards destroyed just about everything at the temple except the T'ang dynasty pillars in the main hall where we were standing, and the Sung dynasty pagoda on the ridge behind the temple. He invited us to join him for some tea and a sweet pudding made from *kuo-pa*, or scorched rice.

While we were eating the pudding, I showed the abbot some of Stonehouse's poems I brought with me and asked him if he had heard of Shih-wu. He hadn't, which didn't surprise me. We chatted for a while, then said good-bye. The day was half over, and we were anxious to find the mountain where Stonehouse spent thirty-five years. We returned to the main road and headed south again. Even though the station manager had pointed the driver in the right direction, for the next hour we must have stopped a dozen times to ask villagers along the roadside if they had heard of Hsiamushan. Some of them had, and one of them finally directed us across some railroad tracks onto a dirt road just wide enough for a single car. The road led to the base of a mountain, and a farmer walking along the road confirmed that the mountain was, indeed, Hsiamushan. We were excited.

One poem that came to mind as we headed up the dirt road was #76 of his *Mountain Poems*, one Stonehouse apparently wrote on the mid-autumn moon festival:

> *A thatch hut is lonely on a new fall night*
> *with white peas in flower and crickets calling*
> *mountain moon silver evokes an old joy*
> *suddenly I've strolled west of the summit*

Abbot Fu-hsing of Wanshou Temple

We figured his hut must have been on the east side of the summit. But we didn't know how close we could get to the top. Our driver's battered blue Polish taxi was having a hard time with the road. The ruts were deep from a recent rain. But the road kept going, and so did his Skoda.

Finally, a few hundred meters short of the summit, a chain barred our way. We had no choice but to stop. We got out and stepped over the chain, walked past a one-story cement building, and continued up the road. It didn't take long to reach the top, but there wasn't much to see. First of all, the bamboo was too high to see the surrounding countryside. Second of all, there were only two things on top besides the bamboo. One was a huge metal dish for relaying electronic signals. The other was a cement bunker. While we were standing there wondering what to do next, six soldiers came running out of the bunker with their rifles pointed at us. Ooops: It was a military installation.

Just then, the officer in charge came huffing up the road from where we had parked the car. Before he had a chance to ask what we were doing here, we explained that we were looking for traces of a monk who lived here 600 years ago. It seemed like a reasonable explanation to us. I took my copy of Stonehouse's poems out of my bag. It was a copy of the bilingual edition I'd published in America six years earlier and included the Chinese along with my translations. I pointed to one of Stonehouse's poems in which he mentioned living on a mountain called Hsiamushan. The officer's eyes opened wide, and he started to read the poems. I told him we thought Stonehouse's hut must have been just east of the summit, and we were hoping to see if there was anything left. The officer surprised us. He waved the soldiers away then pulled out his machete and led us straight into the bamboo. It was a variety known as arrow bamboo and produced the tenderest shoots. But it also grew incredibly thick. He plunged into it anyway and hacked his way through with his machete. We followed. Still, even with him leading the way, the bamboo was so dense, at times we were unable to move our arms or our legs. Somehow, though, we got loose and struggled on.

After about twenty minutes, we finally emerged at a small farmstead. We were covered with scratches and thought the officer might have led us through the bamboo as punishment for entering a restricted area. But in truth, he was trying to help us. He pointed to the farmhouse and said that before the telecommunications station was built, the farmhouse was the only structure on the mountain. Just then, a farmer appeared in the doorway and waved for us to come inside.

The farmer said he had been living here for the past twenty years. He moved here shortly after the Red Guards tore down the other buildings that comprised a small temple that was built next to Stonehouse's hut after he died. Stonehouse said there was a spring behind his hut, and the farmer showed it to us. It was still flowing, just as it was when Stonehouse wrote #55:

> *The Way of the Dharma is too singular to copy*
> *but a well-hidden hut comes close*
> *I planted bamboo in front to form a screen*
> *from the rocks I led a spring into my kitchen*
> *gibbons bring their young to the cliffs when fruits are ripe*
> *cranes move their nests from the gorge when pines turn brown*
> *lots of idle thoughts occur during meditation*
> *I gather the deadwood for my stove*

The farmer's hut was twice as big as Stonehouse's hut, its walls were made of stone not mud, and its roof was now tiled. But the spring still flowed in back, and the slopes were still covered with tea and bamboo, and a couple of pines were still enjoying the breeze. The farmer invited us inside for a cup of tea. He said he lived here alone. His children had grown up, and his wife lived in the village at the foot of the mountain. Like Stonehouse in #183, he didn't have much to say:

> *I built my hut on Hsia Summit*
> *plowing and hoeing make up my day*
> *half a dozen terraced plots*
> *two or three hermit neighbors*
> *I made a pond for the moon*

and sell wood to buy grain
an old man with few schemes
I've told you all that I own

It was with great difficulty that we tore ourselves away and said good-bye to the farmer and the installation commander. But the sun was going down. By the time we returned to Huchou, our driver had to use his headlights. When we entered the bus station to pick up our bags, Mister Kao was still there. He was waiting for us. He said he had arranged for us to spend the night right there. He said the bus station had its own hotel. It even had a name: Bus Station Hotel. It was quite spartan, but why not? Three beds cost 30RMB. How could we refuse? Before Mister Kao headed home, he even gave us directions to one of his favorite restaurants. It was called Tinglienfang and was a ten-minute walk. The walk was worth it. They had the best steamed buns we had ever eaten. Afterwards, we went back to our room, opened a couple beers and watched the moon outside our window rise above the bus station parking lot. It wasn't the Master of Nets Garden in Suchou, but we couldn't have been happier. What a day!

The next morning there was a knock on our door. It was Mister Kao. He said the bus for our next destination left in thirty minutes. It was only 6:30, and we weren't planning on leaving that early, much less getting up. But Mister Kao was in charge of our lives now, and we were grateful. We got our gear together and went out onto the street in front of the bus station and bought some fried bread for breakfast. After coming back to the bus station the night before, we had told Mister Kao our next destination was Mokanshan, a mountain about fifty kilometers south of Huchou. He said he would see if he could arrange something for us. Apparently he did. He said the 6:30 bus would take us to Wukang. He said he called the bus station manager there, and the manager had arranged for a van to take us up the mountain for 100RMB. That wasn't cheap, but we had no choice. Mister Kao said there was only one bus a day to Mokanshan that time of year, and it didn't leave until the afternoon.

Mister Kao was like a travel agent. The previous day he'd arranged for the taxi to take us to the top of Hsiamushan, then arranged for us to spend the night at the bus station hotel, and now he was arranging transportation to our next destination. Before we said good-bye, we walked out to the bus station parking lot and took a picture together with one of the drivers. A few minutes later, we waved our travel agent bodhisattva good-bye.

Thirty minutes later, just as Mister Kao had told us, the bus station manager in Wukang was waiting for us, and so was the van he had hired to take us to Mokanshan. The name was known to every businessman and bureaucrat in the Yangtze Delta. It was where people went to get away from the summer heat, assuming they could afford to take time off from work. We weren't trying to get away from the heat, but we thought we should check it out, if only for future reference.

It was a fall day, a sunny fall day, and it was a beautiful drive through the countryside and into the mountains. By the time we got there, we wished it had taken longer. We were there in less than an hour. Mokanshan was different from the other mountains we had visited. Instead of temples, the mountain was dotted with villas. It was 700 meters above the surrounding countryside, and the surrounding countryside was only a few meters above sea level. During the summer, its slopes were ten degrees centigrade cooler than Suchou or Hangchou or Shanghai.

As we got out of the van, we had to put on our jackets. It was October 23, but the tourist season was already over. We were practically the only guests at the only hotel still open. It was called the Yinshan and was a rambling old place. According to the manager, it had once been the villa of a Shanghai official. He said that most of the villas on the mountain were built by foreigners decades ago but that nowadays they were used to accommodate the employees of various government agencies. His was one of the few hotels open to the public.

Since the day was still young, we took a short hike through the bamboo that surrounded everything. But except for the bamboo-covered slopes that stretched as far as we could see, there wasn't much else. I'm guessing that people enjoyed hiking around the mountain during the summer. But we didn't feel like hiking. We walked back to our hotel and took the day off. After lunch, we even took naps. And after dinner, we sat on the balcony outside our room and watched the moon disappear over the roof of our hotel. It was certainly different from watching the moon from the bus station hotel the previous night. It was quiet. And it was cold. We should have had some whiskey, but all we had was beer. I'm not sure what we were expecting to find on Mokanshan. But whatever it was, it wasn't there.

We left the next morning at seven on the daily bus to Wukang and were there an hour later. From Wukang, we took another bus to Teching. It was only fifteen minutes away, and it was on the train line. Since the train to our next destination didn't leave for two hours, we stashed our bags at the luggage depository and hired a motorized three-wheeler to take us to Leitienchen. In Huchou, Mister Kao had told us Leitienchen was famous for its freshwater pearls, and we decided that would be more interesting than waiting at the train station. We told our driver to take us to the pearls.

We were there in fifteen minutes. But if there were pearls, they were hiding. It was just a village on a canal. When we asked the driver about this, he told us to follow him. After parking his vehicle, he led us into an alley that wound through the village and eventually came out at a pearl factory. It was located along a canal that was filled with wire cages full of oysters. There was no one at the gate, and our driver led us straight into the work area where girls were sitting in pairs on benches. We watched as one of the girls opened an oyster, removed its mantle, and sliced the mantle into tiny squares. Then the other girl picked up the squares with tweezers and inserted them into the oyster. After inserting a dozen or so squares at various points in the oyster's interior, she put the oyster in a basket. Then the two girls repeated the process with the next oyster. Apparently, the pieces of mantle acted as the irritant inside the oyster that caused it to form a pearl.

While we were taking pictures of this process, our pearl factory tour came to a sudden end. The manager stormed in and chased us and our driver out. Apparently, the process was supposed to be a secret.

Huchou bus station bodhisattva and driver

Actually, there was nothing secret about it. We had seen documentary films that showed the process. The factory manager was probably more concerned about the lack of security.

Our driver then led us back to his vehicle. But before we headed back to Teching, I asked him if there was any place in the village where we might buy some pearls. He then led us to the village market. It was a covered area where local farmers brought their produce to sell. It wasn't market day, and the place was nearly deserted. We thought maybe some local entrepreneurs would be selling their own homegrown pearls, but no such entrepreneurs were in sight. While we were wondering why our driver brought us there, he led us to one of the small stores that bordered the covered area. The owner had several necklaces for sale. That was probably why the factory manager chased us out. All the pearls were the property of the factory, and he was probably aware that some of them wandered out from time to time. The owner said the factory had an arrangement with another factory that turned its pearls into jewelry. Local people, she said, weren't supposed to sell pearls to outsiders.

The woman declined to explain how the pearls in her store got there. Presumably, they were smuggled out of the factory, or produced on the sly. In any case, one strand was such a beautiful iridescent pink, and the price was so right, I bought it for my wife. We walked back to our three-wheeler in a happy mood and laughed as we slipped out of Leitien Village and the clutches of the freshwater pearl police.

杭州

18. Hangchou

By the time we got back to Teching and reclaimed our bags, we still had thirty minutes before our train was due. To kill time, we wandered into a store next to the train station. Among the items we couldn't pass up were aluminum-backed pocket mirrors engraved with pictures of Hangchou's famous West Lake. The lake looked so beautiful we bought

Adrift on West Lake

a dozen to give to friends back home. Ninety minutes later, we checked into the Hangchou Overseas Chinese Hotel that overlooked the real thing. When Marco Polo visited Hangchou in the thirteenth century, he described it as the most beautiful city in the world. Taken as a whole, we thought Suchou had maintained more of its traditional charm. But nothing in Suchou could compare with Hangchou's West Lake.

Lots of cities in China had a West Lake, but Hangchou's was the most famous of them all. It wasn't simply the lake itself—which was lovely enough—but its associations. For most of the past thousand years, Hangchou, and not Beijing, has been the cultural capital of China. This is saying a lot, but it's true. A number of years ago, I saw a series of maps of China's dynasties showing population densities in terms of the number of artists, poets, statesmen, and intellectuals of note. According to the maps, the area around Hangchou out-produced all other areas in China beginning in the Sung dynasty a thousand years ago, and the city maintained its prominence until the focus finally shifted to Beijing in the Ch'ing dynasty a mere 300 years ago. With so many poets and artists in residence, it isn't surprising that the city's lake acquired such fame.

Originally, the lake was not a lake but a lagoon formed by the nearby Chientang River. For the people who lived in Hangchou there were two problems with the lagoon. First, its water was too brackish to drink, even during droughts. Second, the tidal bore that came up the Chientang River every fall flowed into the lagoon and often flooded the city. The lake that we saw on our arrival and Marco Polo saw in the thirteenth century was the result of dikes and locks built by a series of governors beginning in the ninth century.

Since it was already past noon, we didn't want to do anything more than enjoy the lake that everyone—including us—came to see. There were a dozen boats waiting for people like us near the promenade in front of our hotel. But first, we supplied ourselves with a few bottles of red wine. We thought we would enjoy the lake in the manner in which it was enjoyed by poets in the past. As luck would have it, we found three bottles of Marco Polo Cabernet waiting for us at our hotel's own convenience store. We had tried a number of wines on our trip, and the Marco

Soaking boats to fix leaks

Polo Cabernet was by far the best. And it was produced right here in Hangchou. We weren't sure where the grapes were from, but we weren't interested. Unfortunately, we later learned that the company went belly up, which explained why finding a bottle was always surprising. Finding three bottles, of course, was really surprising. After leaving one of the bottles in our room for later, we went back out to the promenade and hired a boat for the modest sum of 18RMB per hour. We sat down on the sedan-style seats underneath an awning that shielded us from the sun, and the boatman cast off.

The boatman propelled the boat by using a scull, or single oar, at the stern, sort of like the way a fish uses its tail. We were surprised how fast we went, and how smoothly. We dipped our hands into the water and watched the sunlight dance on the waves, and opened the first bottle of wine. When we asked the boatman if we could try our hand with the scull, he said passengers weren't allowed to do anything but sit and enjoy gliding around the lake, which was what we did.

The boatman, though, had to row somewhere, so we told him to take us to the Island of Little Oceans in the southern part of the lake. The island wasn't there when Marco Polo visited in the thirteenth century. It was made at the beginning of the seventeenth century from silt dredged from the lake bottom. But it wasn't much of an island. The Chinese described it this way: "in the lake there is an island, and in the island there is a lake." There were, in fact, three lakes or small ponds in the middle of the island. The island was not much more than an embankment separating the ponds from each other and from the surrounding lake. The island's most famous sight, though, wasn't its ponds or pavilions or the bridge that zigzagged its way across the ponds. It wasn't on the island. A hundred meters away were three small stone pagodas standing above the water, as if in space. In former times, they were filled with candles at night and looked like apparitions of a floating world.

Our boatman dropped us off on the island, and we worked our way across the bridge to the other side, where we re-boarded our gliding palanquin and headed for an island in the northern part of the lake, at which time we opened the second bottle of wine. The second island was called Pavilion in the Lake, and that was about all it had room for, besides a small teahouse. Like Island of Little Oceans, it was made from lake silt. Despite its diminutive size, musicians performed there at night and were joined by a few boatloads of tourists. As we approached, we told the boatman to keep rowing. We didn't want to do anything other than glide and enjoy our wine, which we did until the sun began to set. The boatman said it was quitting time and rowed back to where we got on. He said the only boats allowed on the lake after sunset were those that took people to the Pavilion in the Lake for the nightly musical performance.

As we left the lake behind, we glided down the street as if we were still in our boat—after two bottles of wine, how could we not? I'm not sure how far we glided, but we eventually realized we needed food, and I recognized one of my favorite signs: Koupuli, or "Dogs Won't Touch 'Em." It was a restaurant chain based in Tienchin, famous for its steamed buns. Their buns were good but not as good as the ones we had in Huchou. We also tried a bottle of Great Wall red wine with our meal. But it wasn't as good as the third bottle of Marco Polo Cabernet. Obviously, we were under the spell of West Lake.

The next morning we recovered earlier than usual and went for a walk along the promenade in front of our hotel. West Lake looked lovely in the fog. It was so calm, the surface of the water was like glass. We had already been out on the lake the day before, but we hadn't seen the sights that surrounded it. We went back to our hotel and rented bicycles. From our hotel we pedaled to the lake's northeast corner, then turned west onto the road that circled the lake. A minute later, we turned off onto Paiti Causeway and followed it to Kushan Island. The causeway was named for the ninth-century poet Pai Chu-yi (772–846), who served as the city's governor. It was Pai who initiated the flood control measures that resulted in the formation of West Lake, and the citizens of Hangchou honored his memory with his own causeway, on top of which was a two-lane road shared by cars, bicycles, and pedestrians alike.

Just past the point where the causeway joined the island, we turned off the road onto a path reserved for pedestrians and bicycles. As we pedaled around the northern part of the island, we found ourselves alone. Everyone seemed to prefer the sights of the island's south shore: the provincial library, the provincial museum, and the city's famous Louwailou restaurant. We were more interested in the man who made the island his home. A minute later, we arrived at his grave. His name was Lin Ho-ching (967–1028), and he lived on the island in the early eleventh century. In fact, for the last twenty years of his life, he never left the island. Nor did he marry or have children. His wives, he said, were the plum trees he planted, and his children were the cranes he trained to dance. One of the birds was his favorite. And when Lin died, the crane died of grief. There was a pavilion near his grave that commemorated their friendship.

After paying our respects, we pedaled on. The fog was beginning to lift, and the sun was beginning to shine through. Before crossing the bridge that reconnected with the lakeshore, we turned back along the island's south shore and pedaled to the front of an archway that announced the presence of the Hsiling Seal Society.

The Chinese have been carving their names on stone and metal and bone for 4,000 years, and there were few possessions more important than a person's seal. Documents were not official without one. Signatures were fine, but they weren't official. Only the seal made something legal. So naturally the design of a seal was something people paid great attention to, especially artists, who often had a dozen or more for different phases of their creative lives or for different kinds of paintings or calligraphy.

The Hsiling Seal Society was founded in the 1920s by four men who wanted to study and preserve the art of seal carving, and they chose this place on Kushan for their get-togethers. After parking our bicycles, we walked through the archway and up the steps to the place where they met. In addition to a garden setting, the society possessed one of China's best collections of seals, hundreds of which were on display. It was overwhelming, and we limited ourselves to simply being amazed at the artistry—which involved adapting the structure of Chinese characters to the shape of a stone. Even a square stone posed challenges. Over the centuries, any given character had multiple forms, hence the carver had to choose among these different forms so that all the characters in a person's name formed one harmonious whole. Of course, there were stones of all sizes and shapes for sale, and visitors could have their name carved for a price. But a good carver usually took days or even weeks to think through the design, and I didn't want one that said "Bill."

We walked back down to our bicycles, pedaled across Hsiling Bridge, and rejoined the main road that skirted the lake's north shore. A hundred meters later, we stopped again at Hangchou's most famous shrine. It was built in the thirteenth century in honor of Yueh Fei. When North China was invaded by nomads in the twelfth century, the Sung dynasty court was forced to flee from its capital in Kaifeng to Hangchou, where it reestablished its capital. Yueh Fei was still a boy then, but he grew up fast. When he was still a young man, he organized an army of peasants and defeated the invaders, and pushed them back across the Yellow River. Unfortunately, the Sung court became fearful of Yueh Fei's intentions and had him executed, after which it promptly lost the territory Yueh Fei had reclaimed.

As we entered the shrine, we stopped behind the statues of four men who were kneeling before a statue of Yueh Fei. The kneeling men were responsible for his death and were now asking for forgiveness. According to the caretaker, the statues had to be replaced from time to time. People sometimes damaged them while expressing their anger. There was now a sign asking them not to do that.

We returned once more to our bicycles and continued on for several kilometers, all the way to the entrance of Lingyin Temple. It was located at the foot of the hills that encircled the lake and was easily the most famous temple in the Hangchou area. After parking our bicycles and paying the admission fee, we walked past a cliff carved with hundreds of buddhas and bodhisattvas. An Indian monk who came here in the fourth century thought the cliff looked a lot like one on a mountain in India, and he called it the Cliff That Flew Here. The statues were carved later in the thirteenth and fourteenth centuries and were still in excellent condition, thanks to Chou En-lai, who ordered the Red Guards to leave them alone. The focal point was a statue of Maitreya Buddha, the one with the big belly. There was a long line of people waiting to climb up beside him for a snapshot. It reminded us of children visiting a department store Santa Claus.

We stood in line, too, and asked Maitreya to make us wiser. I'm still waiting. Afterwards, we entered the temple across from the cliff. Lingyin's fame was well deserved. Everything was big. But the two most impressive features of this impressive temple were the twin pagodas in front of the main shrine hall and the buddha statue inside. The two pagodas had survived fires and wars for the past thousand years, but the buddha statue had only been there since 1956. It was the largest seated statue of the Buddha in China and was carved out of huge blocks of camphor wood. What was so remarkable about it was that the work was done in the middle of Mao's Great Leap Forward. We couldn't help wonder how that happened. Someone at Lingyin Temple must have had really good connections.

After our necks got too stiff to look up anymore at the pagoda or the buddha statue, we returned to our bicycles and considered our next stop.

Buddha rock carving outside Lingyin Temple

We could have taken the cable car to the peak that overlooked West Lake. But we decided to stay at ground level. We pedaled back toward the lake, but halfway there we turned off on Dragon Well Road. I think we must have pedaled five or six kilometers, and half of that was uphill. But we were determined to visit the home of China's most famous green tea.

On the way up the final part of the road, we stopped to catch our breaths and met a local tea grower. His name was Hsu Shun-fu, and he offered to lead us to the well that made the tea famous. It wasn't hard to find, and I suppose we could have found it ourselves, but Mister Hsu wanted to make sure we saw its most unusual feature: when he stirred the water, a line appeared on the surface, danced around a bit, then disappeared. We were mystified until Mister Hsu explained that the water was actually a mixture of well water and stream water of different viscosities. That explained the mystery behind Dragon Well, but it didn't explain the mystery behind the tea.

Mister Hsu anticipated our next question and asked us to follow him to his neighbor's house. Other teas, he said, were picked every few months, but Dragon Well was only picked twice a year, in spring and in fall. And when other teas were harvested, one or two leaves were picked along with the bud. Dragon Well included only the bud just after it opened. And while other teas were dried in the sun, even if only briefly, Dragon Well went straight into a huge charcoal-heated wok, first for fifty minutes, then for twenty-seven minutes and one last time for eighteen minutes, a process we watched at his neighbor's house. But the distinctive flavor of Dragon Well, or Lungching, he said, wasn't due to the drying process as much as it was the soil. The soil in the surrounding hills was extremely sandy, and water didn't stay on the roots long enough to effect the tea. The flavor, he said, came from the sun.

Then he led us back to his house and made us some tea. He said when Dragon Well was first brewed 1,300 years ago, it was used as a medicine for cataracts. It brightened people's eyes. We were too young for cataracts but not too young to feel our eyes brighten. The tea he made for us, he said, came from leaves picked earlier that year in spring. He said they had a subtler flavor than leaves picked in fall. Our first impression

Dragon Well Spring

was one of bitterness, then came a rush of sweetness, and finally our thirst disappeared. He made several infusions from the same leaves, and we stayed until the flavor was gone. What was remarkable was that he didn't try to sell us any tea. He just wanted to share what he knew. And we were glad he did.

We thanked Mister Hsu for his kindness and headed back to the lake refreshed. Fortunately, it was downhill. Just past where the road met the lake again, we stopped at a temple that was being restored. Its name was Chingtzu Temple. As we entered the courtyard, we were surprised at the size of the wood destined to become the temple's new pillars. We wondered where the trees came from. Probably not China. What was equally surprising was that all the workmen were using hand tools— plumb lines, planes, squares, mallets, and handsaws. We didn't see a single power tool, or a single nail.

But the reason we stopped wasn't to watch carpenters at work, it was because a thousand years ago this was Hangchou's most famous temple, even more famous than Lingyin Temple. Over the centuries, it was the home of many famous monks, but the most famous of them all was a monk named Chi-kung, who lived here eight hundred years ago.

In the history of Chinese Buddhism, no other monk has been the subject of so many stories and legends. The theme, though, that runs through all the stories about Chi-kung is that he was wild and crazy and the patron saint of all those who washed away the cares of this world with a sip or two of wine. We figured he had been watching over us, and at the monastery store we bought a puppet in his likeness. All we had to do was pull a string, and he lifted up a gourd of wine. He was our new best friend.

The temple where Chi-kung once lifted up his gourd was located between two mountains. The mountain to the south was where Sung dynasty emperors prayed to Heaven when Hangchou was the country's southern capital. The mountain to the north was more interesting. It was called Hsichaoshan, and it was once the site of Leifeng (Thunder Peak) Pagoda, beneath which lies the most beautiful woman no one wants to see.

The story goes something like this: once upon a time, a handsome young man fell in love with a woman dressed in white. But the woman was really a powerful white snake who wanted to live in the world of humans. Eventually the young man discovered the identity of his lover and asked a Buddhist monk to liberate him from the snake's spell. The battles that followed became the subject of one of the most famous Chinese operas: *The Legend of the White Snake.* According to this story, the monk was finally able to imprison the white snake in the foundation of Leifeng Pagoda. And there she was doomed to remain until West Lake dried up, the Chientang Tidal Bore failed to appear, or the pagoda fell down. Well, the pagoda fell down in 1924. I don't know whether that means White Snake is now among us, but in case she's still under the rubble, the monks at Chingtzu Temple were also rebuilding the pagoda.

Since that was pretty much it for our list of sights to see, we headed back to our hotel, then went to find a place to eat. We decided to try something other than steamed buns and passed up Dogs Won't Touch 'Em. We opted instead for one of the city's oldest restaurants, the Kueiyuankuan, where we filled up on eel and shrimp noodles. The noodles were great. The best noodles we had the entire trip. But we weren't done. On the way back to our hotel, we stopped in a store that sold wine and found two more bottles of Marco Polo Cabernet. We bought both and a few minutes later sat down on the shore of West Lake and toasted all those who had sat there like us over the centuries under the light of the same moon. Where would poets be, we wondered, without the moon, and where would poets be without wine? We didn't wonder long.

紹興

19. Shaohsing

Hangchou was like Suchou. It was the kind of town where there was always something more to see. But we had to be back in Hong Kong in a matter of days, and there were more places on our itinerary. Next up was a city that was even more ancient than Hangchou. It was Shaohsing, and it was only fifty kilometers to the east. We were there by nine o'clock the next morning.

Orchid Pavilion

From the town's bus station, we climbed aboard a three-wheeler and told the driver to take us to the Shaohsing Hotel. Our trip was coming to an end, and we hadn't spent nearly as much money as we had expected. So we decided to indulge. And we were glad we did. The hotel was an island of loveliness and calm in an ugly, noisy city. And it was only 150RMB for a room with a garden view. But we weren't there to spend time in our hotel. We were there to see the sights, and we didn't waste any time venturing forth.

As soon as we dropped our bags in our room, we went back out onto the street and hired another three-wheeler to take us to Kuaichishan. It was four kilometers away at the southeast edge of town, and we were there in minutes. The reason we were there was to pay our respects to Yu the Great. Kuaichishan was where he was buried.

Yu preceded us here by 4,300 years. He was the man who finally figured out how to control the flooding of the Yellow River, which he did by dredging, not by building dikes. He was also the founder of China's first dynasty, the Hsia. Until several decades ago, historians dismissed the Hsia as a myth. But recent excavations in the middle reaches of the Yellow River have dispelled such doubts. The Hsia was real, and so was Yu the Great.

The reason he left the Yellow River and traveled this far south was to meet with leaders of areas newly incorporated into the realm of Han Chinese culture. But soon after he came here, he died. The exact location of his grave was unknown, but it was somewhere on the mountain. Over the centuries, many emperors had come to pay homage, and a number of shrines were built at the foot of the mountain. We visited the latest version and also stopped to look at a huge rock with a hole in it. It was brought here by Yu, but no one seems to know why. The hole reminded us of the moon. Like all rulers of ancient China, Yu was a shaman and a worshipper of the moon goddess, and the hole in his rock was a perfect likeness.

The hole was also a perfect likeness of our stomachs. Another three-wheeler took us back to our hotel, where we had lunch, and afterwards we went for a stroll on the hill behind the hotel. It was called Fushan

Yu the Great grave memorial

Hill, and it was also connected, more or less, with Yu the Great. As China's mythic past became its historic past, Shaohsing became the capital of the state of Yueh, whose rulers were descended from the wife of Yu the Great. In return for their allegiance, Yu gave his in-laws the area around Shaohsing as their fief. Around 500 BC, Kou Chien became King of Yueh and eventually made Yueh the dominant power south of the Yangtze. His palace was on Fushan, right where we were strolling. The hill was now a park. It was a nice park, though, and from the top we had a panoramic view of the city. The view, however, was depressing.

We weren't alone in such an assessment. Kou Chien also found life in Shaohsing depressing, and he built a retreat thirteen kilometers southwest of town. In addition to amusing himself in other pursuits, he grew orchids. And his retreat became known as Lanting, or Orchid Pavilion. The orchids were long gone, but there was something else that attracted our interest. We walked back down the hill and hired another three-wheeler. Thirty minutes later, we arrived at Orchid Pavilion's modern incarnation.

In addition to ponds, pavilions, and a shrine to China's greatest calligrapher, the place included China's only calligraphy museum. The Chinese have always appreciated a good piece of calligraphy more than a good painting, and we went inside. Calligraphy reveals a person's character better than a painting, if only because a person doing calligraphy can't think of anything else while they're doing it. It's like being a dancer on the dance floor. The Chinese have always considered it their greatest art. And, of course, the museum included the greatest piece of calligraphy by the greatest of all calligraphers.

The man's name was Wang Hsi-chih (303–361), and he came here with forty friends on the third day of the third lunar month in the year 353 AD. The Chinese reserved that day for ridding themselves of evil influences by bathing in a clear stream and getting drunk. Nowadays, the Chinese celebrate the day by visiting ancestral graves, and call it Grave Sweeping Day. But its ancient roots involved communication with the spiritual world, which required ritual purification, not to mention wine. With that in mind, Wang and his friends came to Orchid

Pavilion, got drunk, and communed with the muse of poetry. They sat along the banks of a small winding stream and played a game that was first played 400 years earlier along the Chuchiang Waterway near the ancient capital of Ch'ang-an.

The rules were simple: everyone sat along a stream with ink and brush. A jug of wine was placed in a miniature boat and allowed to drift down the stream. Whenever the jug reached a participant, he had to take a drink and add a line of verse or even a whole poem to the scroll of paper. During the course of this particular party, the forty-one participants at Orchid Pavilion produced thirty-seven poems. And when they were done, they asked Wang to write a preface. It was the most beautiful piece of calligraphy ever produced by the man whom the Chinese have ever since called their greatest calligrapher.

His preface consisted of only 324 characters and probably took no more than twenty or thirty minutes to write. But even Wang recognized it as the finest piece he had ever done. It became a treasured heirloom, and was handed down from one generation to the next for seven generations until the T'ang dynasty. The founder of the T'ang was a great collector of Wang Hsi-chih's work, and he simply had to have the Orchid Pavilion Preface, as it was called. When his officials found out who had it, they got the owner drunk, stole the calligraphy, and brought it back to the emperor—who considered it one of his greatest treasures. Before he died, he ordered that Wang's calligraphy accompany him to the grave. And that's where it still is, as the emperor's tomb has yet to be opened. Fortunately, in the centuries before it disappeared, a number of copies were made, and we saw facsimiles for sale. But as lovely as the place was, everyone was sober. We were, too, alas. We were also hungry again.

We resolved this crisis by returning to Shaohsing and looking for a place to eat. A few inquiries later found us sitting down in a restaurant fifty meters west of our hotel's north gate. The name of the place was the Yuanlin, and it was delightful. The owner brought a table outside so we could dine alfresco in the adjacent park. Then he brought out the food. The chestnuts in anise were memorable, so was the carp cooked

Shaohsing wine containers

in Shaohsing's famous rice and millet wine. Before we went to bed, we resolved to find out more about Shaohsing wine in the morning.

We didn't have to look very far. The city's brewers had been perfecting their wine for at least 2,500 years. When Kou Chien wanted to rouse his army, he had barrels of this wine dumped into a stream and ordered his soldiers to drink the water. Afterwards, he ordered them to march north and attack the neighboring state of Wu, whose capital was Suchou, which they did. Nor did the fame of Shaohsing wine go unnoticed by the first Westerners who traveled to China. Following his visit to the Middle Kingdom in the early fourteenth century, Friar Odoric told his fellow Italians that Shaohsing wine was every bit as good as fine Spanish sherry. Not to be outdone, we hired a guide, and at nine o'clock the next morning, we followed the good friar's footsteps into the Shaohsing Laochiu Winery. Shaohsing wine is called *lao-chiu*, or old wine, because, unlike most rice wine, it's aged.

Our guide poured us each a glass of the winery's amber brew and explained how it's made. First, there's the water. Only the mineral-rich water of nearby Chienhu Lake is used. This is then combined with glutinous rice from neighboring Kiangsu province and millet from North China. The resulting mixture goes through two fermentations, the first lasting a week and the second more than a month. The mash is then pressed, and the resulting wine is pasteurized and aged in pottery jars for as long as ten or even twenty years. Our guide poured us another glass and explained that Shaohsing wine is also good for the health. It contains, she said, twenty-one amino acids. She didn't explain how those amino acids survived the pasteurization process, but we didn't care.

The winery, she said, produced 43,000 tons per year, 60 percent of which was exported to Japan, home of Asia's other famous rice wine, sake. But unlike sake's lighter shades that contain maybe a hint of yellow, Shaohsing wine ranges from amber to red to dark brown, with its color and taste depending on the relationship of glutinous rice to millet. The variation results in four categories of wine, ranging from dry to sweet. After pouring us glasses of each kind, our guide explained that the fame of Shaohsing wine rested not only on its taste but also on its medicinal value: it whet the appetite, it relaxed the muscles, it stimulated the circulation, it extended one's life, it did everything except the laundry. But we had to drink it, she said, every day. That sounded like a prescription we could follow, and we bought enough on the way out to extend our lives at least a few days.

After thanking our guide, we floated to our next destination: a small garden at the south edge of town. It was called Shen Garden, and it was once a favorite place for local poets to meet. Among them was one of the most famous poets of the twelfth century. His name was Lu You (1125–1210), and everyone in Shaohsing, if not all of China, knows the story of how Lu You married his cousin, T'ang Wan, and how he was forced to divorce her because his mother didn't like her distracting him from his studies. Lu and his cousin then remarried other people, but years later they met by chance one day in Shen Garden. Before parting, they both wrote poems to each other on the garden wall. T'ang Wan died the following year, of grief, people say, and visitors can still read the couple's poems in the garden's small memorial hall. I read Lu You's, which was composed to the tune *Chaitoufeng*:

> *Your plain pink hands*
> *this fragrant yellow wine*
> *the city in spring the willows by the temple walls*
> *the cruelty of the east wind*
> *the fading of our joy*
> *the constant thoughts of sorrow*
> *all the years apart*
> *and yet and yet and yet again*
> *spring is still the same*
> *though you're thinner now*
> *the tear-streaked red eyes behind silken sleeves*
> *the peach petals falling*
> *the deserted pond pavilion*
> *the vows that remain*
> *the letters we can't send*
> *no and no and no again*

It was always hard visiting such beautiful places that were home to so much sadness. We left the garden and walked a few more blocks to a place associated with a more recent author. It was the home of Lu Hsun. Lu Hsun was born here in 1881, and he also grew up here. The part of the house in which he lived was preserved as if he were expected back. The furniture was the same. Even the garden where he wrote some of his most memorable essays was still here. Next door, there was a memorial hall, where people came to pay their respects. Mao called Lu China's greatest revolutionary writer. The displays certainly emphasized his left-wing sympathies, but Lu was hardly a revolutionary. Still, he inspired revolutionaries. We also visited the small private school he attended as a boy. It was about a block from his house and was called the Sanweiyuan, or Three Flavor Academy. We could still see Lu Hsun's old desk and the place on it where he carved the character 早 for "early" to remind himself not to be late.

Former quarry of East Lake

One final stop on the Lu Hsun pilgrimage was the old Prosperity Tavern that was once managed by one of his relatives and also appeared in his stories. It was just down the street from the Lu Hsun Memorial Museum, and it was as good a place as any to sit down and enjoy a late lunch. We ordered all the specialties: roast beans in anise, soy sauce duck, drunken shrimp and mushrooms, and, of course, some *lao-chiu*. Before we knew it the afternoon was half over, and so were we. But we weren't quite done with Shaohsing.

We staggered out onto the street and flagged down yet another three-wheeler, and went to see one of Shaohsing's newest sights. It was called East Lake. The lake was the new part. Over 2,000 years ago, the site was used as a quarry and connected with the Grand Canal. Then, about 200 years ago, the local authorities built a dike separating the quarry from the canal, but they continued to allow the canal's water to flow through the quarry by means of a series of locks. The lake they created wasn't more than two meters deep, if that, but it was a stunning setting.

It would have been perfect for a picnic. Unfortunately, we arrived a little late in the day. In fact, we arrived just before closing. But there was still enough time for a boatman to pole us around in one of the long, narrow boats Shaohsing is famous for. He poled us into a series of gorges that snaked into the quarry a hundred meters or so. It was a strange sensation, sort of like floating through a cave that's open at the top. We should have come earlier, or the place should have stayed open later. We had to leave after only an hour, when it finally got too dark to tell the water from the sky. We returned to our hotel and had another memorable dinner at the Yuanlin and went to sleep. Shaohsing was one of the ugliest, most chaotic towns we had been in. But thanks to its wine, we were entranced and wished we could have stayed longer, much longer.

天台

20. Tientai

We didn't feel a thing when we went to bed, but we did the next morning. Despite its reputed health-giving benefits, Shaohsing wine was still wine. We got up slowly. But at least we got up. And at least we made it to the bus station. We had one more mountain to see, and we were there in three hours—or at least near enough. We were still a three-wheeler ride away.

Fengkan Bridge and Sui dynasty wall

As far as mountains in China go, the fame of Tientaishan is fairly recent. It didn't become known to China's literati until Sun Ch'o visited in the middle of the fourth century and wrote a long poetic exposition in praise of its scenic beauty in his "Ode to Visiting Tientaishan." But its real fame didn't begin until the monk Chih-yi moved here near the end of the sixth century.

We met Chih-yi briefly at the beginning of our journey when we visited Hengshan. Chih-yi studied there with the monk Hui-ssu. It was Hui-ssu who established Hengshan as a center of Buddhist practice. Before that, it was a Taoist mountain. His disciple Chih-yi did the same with Tientai. Among the many temples Chih-yi built on the mountain, the most famous was Kuoching. It was located at the foot of the mountain, and we asked our driver to take us there. Kuoching was also the monastery where Han-shan, or Cold Mountain, lived when he wasn't living in his cave. We were there in five minutes. It was that close. The temple had been rebuilt many times, but its original front wall—built to keep out ghosts—was still standing. It was the same wall Cold Mountain covered with poems 1,200 years ago. The graffiti was gone, but the wall was still there. So was the bridge named for Feng-kan, a monk who rode into the temple one day in the eighth century on the back of a tiger. Feng-kan was also known for his abrupt manner. The only thing he would tell anyone who asked for instruction was: "Whatever works 隨意." He also left behind four poems, the first of which is this one:

> *I've been to Tientai*
> *maybe a million times*
> *like a cloud or river*
> *drifting back and forth*
> *roaming free of trouble*
> *trusting the Buddha's spacious path*
> *meanwhile the world's forked mind*
> *only brings people pain*

Tientaishan pagoda

One day when Feng-kan was walking on a nearby slope, he found a child who had been abandoned on the side of the trail. He picked the boy up and brought him back to the monastery. Because of how he was found, people called the boy Shih-te, meaning Pickup, and the monks put him to work in the monastery kitchen. Some years later, the third member of Chinese Buddhism's famous trio showed up. Apparently, he was on the wrong side of the An Lu-shan Rebellion and preferred anonymity. No one ever learned his real name. He called himself Han-shan, or Cold Mountain, after the cave where he lived when he wasn't staying at Kuoching.

Feng-kan, Shih-te, and Han-shan marched to a different drummer. At Kuoching they harassed the monks as well as the pilgrims. Their harassment was harmless enough and was limited to the odd poem they wrote on walls or trees or wherever a passerby would notice. Among Pickup's was #33:

> *We slip into Tientai caves*
> *we visit people unseen*
> *me and my friend Cold Mountain*
> *eat magic mushrooms under the pines*
> *we talk about the past and present*
> *and sigh at the world gone mad*
> *everyone going to Hell*
> *and going for a long long time*

We were hoping to meet this trio of bodhisattvas ourselves, or at least pay our respects. And we hoped to use Kuoching as our base. After crossing Fengkan Bridge and maneuvering past the temple's Sui dynasty wall, we walked through the entrance and asked directions to the guest hall. A few minutes later, we were there. So was the guest manager. This time, I didn't have to roll up my sleeves. We said we wanted to spend a couple of nights, and the guest manager asked his assistant to lead us to the guest wing. That was easy. The guest manager's assistant turned us over to the laywoman in charge of guest quarters, and she showed us to the loveliest of rooms at the back of the temple. All the furniture was rosewood, or at least it looked like rosewood. We were expecting something more rustic, but we weren't complaining. We dropped off our bags, then went to explore the temple.

Kuoching was one of the oldest and best-preserved monasteries in China. The courtyards were vast, and the shrine halls were ancient. The trees were even more ancient. They included thousand-year-old gingkos and locusts and a plum tree that was even older. The laywoman in charge of guest quarters wanted to make sure we saw the plum tree, and took us there first. It was planted by Chih-yi 1,400 years ago. She said it still flowered every spring.

Chih-yi did more than build temples and plant trees. He also established a variety of Buddhism that was much more eclectic than other schools. It admitted the truth of seemingly contradictory teachings by assigning them to different periods of the Buddha's life and by relating them to the different needs of the Buddha's audiences. As far as his own doctrine, Chih-yi and his successors emphasized that every thought of every being was no different from the mind of the Buddha, that our everyday life was the necessary foundation of the religious life. Two hundred years after Chih-yi died, the ninth patriarch of the Tientai sect went even further. He proclaimed that the buddha nature, the ability to become enlightened, was not only shared by all beings, it was shared by mountains and rivers. He could have added plum trees.

Despite the openness of such an approach, the Tientai sect never attracted many adherents in China, and it probably would have disappeared as a distinct teaching if Japanese and Korean monks hadn't been impressed with its equal emphasis on faith and meditation and hadn't taken it back to their lands in the T'ang and Sung dynasties.

After walking through the temple's courtyards, we went back out the front gate and past the Sui dynasty wall and back across Fengkan Bridge and followed a path on the other side of the road that took us through the woods to the stupa containing the remains of the eighth-century monk Yi-hsing. As the result of his writings, Yi-hsing was considered a patriarch of Tantric Buddhism in both China and Japan. He was even more famous as a mathematician, and he was commissioned by the emperor to prepare a new calendar—which he did by setting up celestial observation posts as far south as Vietnam and as far north as Siberia. Being an open-minded scholar he traveled throughout the realm seeking advice. At one point, he visited Kuoching Temple and through an open doorway heard a monk working the beads of an abacus. Yi-hsing was so impressed with the monk's mathematical abilities that he studied with him for several years before finally completing the new calendar. He later died at Kuoching, and was buried on the hill across from the temple.

After paying our respects, we walked farther up the slope to the Sui dynasty pagoda. It was the first thing people saw when they arrived at the foot of the mountain. At sixty meters, it was hard to miss. It was constructed at the beginning of the seventh century shortly after Kuoching was built. We never did find out whose remains it contained. The sun was beginning to set, and we hurried back to the temple. It was a good thing we did. We arrived just in time for dinner. Afterwards we talked to a layman who lived at the temple and who helped take care of guests. His name was Layman Fang, and we asked him if he could help us arrange a three-wheeler for the next day. We wanted to see the sights, both on the mountain and beyond. He said he would take care of it, and he did.

The next morning our three-wheeler was waiting for us in the temple parking lot, and we climbed aboard. We had a big day planned and began with the mountain and Chih-yi. From Kuoching, we followed the main road up the mountain about fifteen minutes, then turned off and zigzagged up the slope on the right until we came to Chenchueh Temple. It was a small temple, but it was an important stop on the pilgrim trail. It contained Chih-yi's mummified remains. We went inside and lit some incense in the shrine hall where his body was kept. We were surprised to find ourselves alone, except for an old monk who served as the caretaker. While the incense burned down, we walked outside to a balcony behind the temple where we had a clear view of the mountain. Tientai was the kind of mountain where a person could get lost. There were so many peaks and ridges and deep valleys. We were glad someone built a road. And we made good use of it. We returned to our three-wheeler, and fifteen minutes later we

Transport to Cold Mountain Cave

arrived at the last stop on our mountain pilgrimage. It was one of China's most famous waterfalls and was called Stone Bridge Cascade.

We got out and walked over to see it for ourselves. Two streams came together just above the waterfall, then flowed under a natural rock bridge before dropping nearly fifty meters into a pool below. There was a restraining barricade near the bridge, but in ancient times some visitors tested their karma by walking across. The great Ming dynasty travel-diarist Hsu Hsia-k'o, whose home and grave we'd visited near Wuhsi, walked out onto the bridge, looked down, and lived to write about it. We decided to limit ourselves to a more distant view. The rock bridge that Hsu and others walked across was a meter wide at its widest point and a half-meter wide at its narrowest. And it was ten meters across and wet with mist from the waterfall. We were happy to turn down the thrill of adventure. Standing there watching the water crash onto the rocks below was enough. We returned to our three-wheeler and went back down the mountain. This time we passed Kuoching Temple by. Our next stop was Cold Mountain's cave.

Cold Mountain Cave

Unlike others who wrote poems on paper or silk and made copies for friends, Cold Mountain wrote his poems on walls or rocks or trees and left them for the wind and rain to sort out. Not long after he disappeared in the early ninth century, a local magistrate collected more than 300 of his poems, and in 1983, I published an English translation of the whole collection. Ever since then, I had wanted to visit the place that inspired the poems.

Our three-wheeler took us back through Tientai, then north on the highway that led toward Shaohsing. After two or three kilometers, we turned west at the Koshan bus stop and followed a dirt road into the countryside. After about twenty minutes, we passed through the village of Pingchiao, and after another twenty, we entered the village of Chiehtou. Halfway through the village, we turned south and followed a stream through a gap in the mountains. On the other side of the mountains, we came to a bridge lined with cormorants drying their wings. We crossed the bridge and followed the road to the left. A few bumpy minutes later, we parked next to a plank bridge that spanned a small stream.

View from inside Cold Mountain Cave

We got out and crossed the bridge, and walked into a narrow ravine. This was Mingyen, or Bright Cliff, where Pickup reportedly lived after leaving Kuoching. We followed the ravine until it ended in a series of huge caverns. A crack between two of them was where Cold Mountain and Pickup reportedly disappeared. At least that was the story.

The first time Cold Mountain tried to visit this same place, he wrote poem #9:

> *I longed to visit the eastern cliff*
> *countless years until today*
> *I finally grabbed a vine and climbed*
> *but met mist and wind halfway*
> *the trail was too narrow for my clothes*
> *the moss too slick for my shoes*
> *I stopped beneath this cinnamon tree*
> *and slept with a cloud for a pillow*

View from outside Cold Mountain Cave

We were glad we had an easier time and lit some incense at the small shrine below the crack where the two eccentric bodhisattvas disappeared. Since there wasn't much else to see, we returned to our three-wheeler and headed for our final destination, the cave where Cold Mountain lived in inspired seclusion. We re-crossed the bridge where the cormorants were still sunning themselves, but instead of heading back to Chiehtou, we turned left and followed the road that followed the river upstream. A sign on the bridge called it the Shihfeng River. We drove for several kilometers along its shore until we came to a village of maybe a dozen houses. It was called Houyen, or Rear Cliff. Our driver turned off the main road and drove through the village. The houses were so close together, our three-wheeler barely fit. It was slow going, but we made it. Once beyond the village, we re-crossed the river and continued on a road that was no more than a pair of ruts. After a kilometer or so, we came to a huge cliff with a huge cave at its base. The cliff was called Hanyen, or Cold Cliff, and the cave was Cold Mountain Cave.

As we got out and started up the trail to the cave, the farmers working the nearby slope stopped to see who would visit such an isolated place. They were harvesting corn, tea, and sweet potatoes. We waved, and they waved back, as we continued up the slope to the cave entrance. The cave faced south, just as I had imagined, toward the course of the sun and the moon. At the entrance, we met the self-appointed caretaker, Mister Yeh. He said he had lived all his life in the village of Yenchien, or Front Cliff. When we asked where that was, he pointed beyond where we had parked. All we could see were two very sad-looking houses. That was all that was left of the village. He said he moved into the cave five years earlier because he liked the quiet. He led us inside to see the shrines someone had set up around the rear walls. The cave was huge and had a high ceiling, and there was lots of bat guano on the dusty rock floor. We lit incense at each of the shrines, just in case one of them "worked."

Afterwards, Mister Yeh led us back to the mouth of the cave where he had built a house out of bricks—but only the walls. There was no roof, and no need for one. The cave supplied the roof. He told us to sit down on the benches that flanked the only table in his roofless house, while he started heating water for noodles. We hadn't had lunch, so we were glad to have something to eat. While he was cooking, he said there used to be a big temple down below where the farmers were harvesting corn. It was gone, and if the Red Guards left something, it wasn't visible. He said he and the other farmers still dug up temple tiles in the fields.

The noodles were just what we needed, especially with the addition of some red pepper paste. We thanked Mister Yeh and left some money where we thought he would find it later. We returned to our three-wheeler and drove back to Kuoching. On the way back, I wrote this poem:

> *Sitting inside Cold Mountain Cave*
> *reading Cold Mountain poems*
> *the sound of hoes turning the earth*
> *old monk bones feeding the corn*

寧波

21. Ningpo

We had one more city to go: Ningpo. But because we wanted to make a stop on the way, we took the slow bus that took the slow road. We had to go via Fenghua and change buses there. Finally, five hours after leaving Tientai, we arrived in Hsikou.

Earlier on our trip, we visited the hometown of Mao Tse-tung. Now that our travels were nearing their end, we wanted to have a look at the

Tienyiko Garden

other end of China's political spectrum: the hometown of Chiang Kai-shek. Ever since Chiang fled to Taiwan together with several million of his fellow Mainlanders, his hometown hadn't exactly been a hotbed of tourism. But times had changed. Once Beijing decided to pursue a policy of reconciliation with Taiwan, Hsikou was spruced up and opened to the curious, which included us.

Chiang was born here in 1887 to a family that could trace its local ancestry back twenty-seven generations to the thirteenth century. From the bus station, we walked down the road that led past the ancestral shrine hall once used by all the clans in this area—including the Chiang clan. The shrine hall was rebuilt in 1986, not long after Beijing and Taipei representatives began meeting secretly in Singapore to begin the long road to reconciliation. It was no coincidence that Taipei's representative in those secret meetings was Chiang Kai-shek's grandson, Chiang Hsiao-wu.

The ancestral shrine hall was now a museum. But aside from a beautifully carved sedan chair used to carry brides to their weddings and an exhibition of local handicrafts, there wasn't much to see. We continued on. Just past the museum was Hsikou's ornamental Wuling Gate, which marked the entrance into the old part of town. A side path led off to two houses on a rocky promontory overlooking the Shan River. The first house was a replica of the house built here by Chiang Kai-shek in 1924 for his third wife Sung Mei-ling, known to the world as Madame Chiang Kai-shek. Next to her house was another house where Chiang Kai-shek's eldest son, Chiang Ching-kuo, lived with his Russian wife, following his return from Moscow in 1937. It was ironic that their houses should be next to one another. When he was in Moscow, Chiang Ching-kuo repudiated the anti-leftist road his father took—which also involved divorcing Chiang Ching-kuo's mother and marrying Sun Yat-sen's sister-in-law. But the irony didn't last long. Two years after Chiang Ching-kuo's return, both his and his stepmother's houses were blown to smithereens by the Japanese.

Another fifty meters down the road was the Chiang ancestral home. It, too, had been rebuilt by the Communist government as part of its

Madame Chiang Kai-shek's house on the Shan River

effort to mend fences with the Nationalists on Taiwan. If the restoration was anything like the original, it served to emphasize the difference between Chiang's upbringing and that of Mao. They were clearly from different classes. Another fifty meters past the old family home was the building where Chiang was born. He was born on the second floor. The first floor was where his father and grandfather carried on the salt business that financed Chiang's education and early political career.

More interesting than the dwellings associated with the Chiang family were the adjacent alleys. Hsikou was a town where people still engaged in country crafts, some of which we saw in the Hsikou Museum. But that was about it. We had seen what we came to see and walked back to the bus station. After reclaiming our bags, we waited for the next bus to Ningpo and had some noodles while we waited. An hour later, we were off, and an hour later we were in downtown Ningpo.

Although Ningpo is now overshadowed by Shanghai, in ancient times it was the major port in East China, while Shanghai was just a small fishing village. Ningpo was where junks from Southeast Asia unloaded their cargoes for transshipment by smaller boats capable of navigating the shallower waters of Hangchou Bay and the Yangtze. Shipping was in the city's blood, and it wasn't a surprise that the world's leading shipping tycoon of the previous few decades was a native of Ningpo, namely Sir Y.K. Pao.

But we arrived by bus, not boat. And we arrived late in the day and in need of a hotel. Most of the hotels that accepted foreigners were located just north of the bus station, so we didn't have far to walk. We tried several of the nicer ones but were put off by their high prices—which averaged over 250RMB, or $50 a night. Finally, we managed to pry loose a room at the Seaman's Hotel, where a whole suite cost a modest 100RMB. We told the desk clerk we were seamen, and he didn't ask to see our papers. I'm guessing they didn't have many guests.

Since the sun was going down, as soon as we dropped our bags in our room, we thought we would have dinner and go to bed early. We were tired and decided to try the hotel restaurant. Eating in hotel restaurants was always a gamble, but this time we hit the jackpot. First, there were fish fillets wrapped in seaweed and deep-fried in batter. Then there was goose liver sausage soaked in anise and Shaohsing wine, then steamed and fried and cut into slices. And it all went down very nicely with half a dozen ice-cold Ningpo beers.

Putting an end to the day early for a change gave us a chance to wash our clothes and catch up on our journals. The next morning, we were ready to see the sights. And they began just a few blocks north of our hotel. Our first stop was the Tienyiko, the Pavilion of Heavenly Oneness. We had already seen a few gardens in Suchou, and we thought they were nice. But they were also tourist sites. The garden that surrounded Ningpo's Tienyiko immediately became our favorite. We found ourselves practically alone. Maybe it was because the Tienyiko wasn't known for its garden. Its principal claim to fame was its library, which was begun by an official in the sixteenth century. The official built a building to house his collection of books. And of course the building had to have a couple of ponds and pavilions. Before long, the place put the gardens of Suchou to shame. Still, nobody talked about the Tienyiko's wonderful layout and architecture. They talked about its books.

At one time, the collection surpassed 70,000 volumes, many of which were rare editions that had been out of print for centuries. In fact, when the Ch'ing dynasty court decided to produce its monumental set of 3,500 standardized literary works—the *Ssukuchuanshu*—it based its arrangement upon the system developed at the Tienyiko Library. The court also called on the Tienyiko to supply a number of missing titles. Over the years, the library's collection had dwindled, especially in recent years. Still, it was a rare chance to see some of the oldest printed books in the world, and in such a beautiful setting. Naturally, we lingered. Other than the Tienyiko, there wasn't anything else we wanted to see in Ningpo. But there were other sights. The other sights, though, were farther afield, east and west of the city.

We decided to begin with the west. Since we were saving so much money on our room, we indulged in a taxi. We asked the driver to take us to the Liangchu Cemetery, which was where China's Romeo and

Juliet were buried. It was only ten kilometers away, and we were there in twenty minutes.

The boy's name was Liang Shan-po, and the girl's name was Chu Ying-t'ai. They were buried here 1,600 years ago, back when the Huns were sacking Rome. Chu Ying-t'ai had a lot in common with Shaohsing's revolutionary heroine, Ch'iu Chin. Bored with conventional life, Chu dressed up as a man and traveled from Ningpo to Hangchou to study. On her way, she met Liang Shan-po, who was also traveling to Hang-chou to study. The two agreed to attend classes together, and they studied together for three years. Chu Ying-t'ai, however, maintained her male disguise, and Liang Shan-po had no idea his closest friend was a woman.

After three years, Chu was finally called back home by her parents, and her parting with Liang remains a favorite scene of Chinese drama, as she tries but fails to convey the true nature of her feelings for her fellow classmate. It wasn't until several years later, when Liang visited Chu in Ningpo, that he discovered she was a woman. When he did, he immediately proposed marriage. But he was too late. Her parents had betrothed her to another. Liang died of a broken heart and was buried where we were standing. Not long after that, Chu was on her way to be married, when she passed by Liang's grave. She stopped the bearers carrying her sedan chair. She ran to Liang's grave and asked the gods to open the grave so that she could join him in death. The gods granted her wish. The tomb opened, then closed around her. Then it reopened, and two butterflies flew out. We were suckers for such stories. But it was too late in the year for butterflies, and after paying our respects we headed back to Ningpo.

As we returned to the city, we told our driver to keep going. Once again, we didn't have to go far. Twenty kilometers east of Ningpo, we pulled into the parking lot of Ayuwang Temple. Since we weren't sure how long we were going to spend there, we paid our driver and figured we would deal with our transportation needs when we were done.

The *a-yu* in Ayuwang was the ancient Chinese transliteration of Ashoka, the name of the king who ruled India in the third century BC. After uniting India in a series of bloody military campaigns, King

99-year-old monk at Ayuwang Temple

Ashoka was converted to Buddhism. As a demonstration of his new faith, he ordered his officials to erect stupas throughout his kingdom, each containing a relic of the religion's founder, Shakyamuni Buddha. In the course of the following centuries, most of Ashoka's stupas were destroyed or forgotten when the subcontinent was swept by a series of foreign invaders. But around the end of the third century AD, the contents of one of the stupas was brought to China by ship, and the port of Ningpo was as far as it got. A propitious place was chosen east of the city, and a pagoda was erected to house the relic.

A temple soon grew up around the pagoda, and the Buddha's relic was later moved inside the temple for safekeeping. Somehow, the temple has managed to hold onto its precious treasure, and hundreds of pilgrims still come here every day to view the relic in its jewel-studded crystal case. We entered the shrine hall to see for ourselves and lit some incense along with the other pilgrims. Behind the crystal case, there was also a reclining statue of the Buddha covered in gold silk representing Shakyamuni as he entered Nirvana. Following his Nirvana, his body was cremated, and his bone chips and ashes were divided among eight kingdoms. Two hundred years later, King Ashoka further divided those remains, and as luck would have it, a piece of the Buddha's skull made it to Ningpo's Ayuwang Temple. It was a beautiful temple in a beautiful setting. Even the modern two-story hotel next door somehow blended in. The hotel provided pilgrims with a place to spend the night.

As we stood there before the piece of the Buddha's skull with our fellow pilgrims, I was reminded of an incident in chapter five of the *Diamond Sutra* where the Buddha decides to test the understanding of one of his disciples. He asks Subhuti, "Can you see the Buddha's bodily form?" And Subhuti answers, "No, World-Honored One, the Buddha's bodily form cannot be seen, because, as the Buddha has taught, bodily form is not bodily form." To which the Buddha adds, "Since whatever has form is empty, when you see a form as having no form you see the Buddha." And so we paid our respects before the formless body of the Buddha.

Afterwards, we continued meandering through the temple's labyrinth of shrine halls and courtyards, and in one of the courtyards, we met

Tientung Temple

Master Heng-yueh. He was wearing the red and yellow robes of a senior monk and was surrounded by a group of disciples. He also had a long, white beard. As soon as he saw us, he walked over and grabbed our arms. He said our beards were longer than his, and he wanted a photo with me and Finn. One of his disciples tried to sneak into the shot, but Heng-yueh shoved him away. Afterwards, he excused himself for not being able to shove his disciple harder. He said he felt weak ever since he celebrated his 99th birthday. Then he went over and gave the same disciple another shove, and both of them burst out laughing.

After the two monks left, we put our cameras away and walked over to the vegetarian restaurant the temple operated for visitors. It was the standard menu of dishes made from soy and wheat gluten products and flavored to taste like meat. It was simple fare, but it was good. Afterwards, we walked back out to the highway. Instead of returning to Ningpo, we walked a hundred meters down the highway to the side road that led to Tientung Temple. There was a bus stop, and thirty minutes later, we were on a bus.

Interior corridor of Tientung Temple

The road wound up into the mountains and at some point passed a pagoda. When we asked one of our fellow passengers about the pagoda, he said it was built in the T'ang dynasty and contained the bones of a large snake. The snake terrorized villagers in the area until it died after eating some steamed buns that turned out to be cobblestones metamorphosed by the magic powers of a monk who lived at Tientung Temple. An hour after we got on the bus, it dropped us off at the entrance of a pine-lined roadway that led to the temple. Fifteen minutes later, we were at the temple's front steps.

Tientung Temple was first built around 300 AD, about the same time as Ayuwang Temple. But while Ayuwang was built for Buddhist pilgrims, Tientung was built for monks who wanted to concentrate on their meditation practice. In fact, it was once one of the five most famous Zen monasteries in China and at one time was home to several thousand monks.

We had already visited Chenju Temple on Yunchushan. But during its heyday, Tientung was even more famous among Zen practitioners, as it was where many of Japan's famous Zen masters studied when they came to China, monks such as Dogen. The monastery was surrounded by pine-covered slopes on three sides, and the buildings were in superb condition, despite their age.

Somehow, we managed to find our way through the labyrinth of corridors to the rear of the complex where they still had a wonderful set of stone carvings of the eighteen Buddhist worthies known as *arhats*. We had never seen a set made of stone before. Usually they were wood or clay. We lit some incense, then headed back out. We were on our own this time. There was no Eccentric Buddha to guide us around. There were over a hundred monks in residence at Tientung, and most of the monastery was off-limits. Once we saw what we could, we walked back down the tree-lined road that brought us there and caught the last bus of the day back to Ningpo. Our trip was almost over. We were down to our last day.

普陀山

22. Putuoshan

We got up at six the next morning and were at the Ningpo ship terminal by seven. We had tickets for the 7:30 to Putuoshan. We had already visited Chiuhuashan, the home of Ti-tsang, the Bodhisattva of Great Vows. Putuoshan was the island home of Kuan-yin, the Bodhisattva of Great Compassion. Of all the destinations of pilgrims in China, Putuoshan was by far the most popular, and our ship was packed.

Taking a break on Putuoshan

As we pulled out of the harbor, our fellow passengers lined the railings. For the first hour, we cruised down the Yung River past hundreds of factories and piers. Finally, the river carried us past the protective breakwater and out into the East China Sea. A roller coaster of waves suddenly jolted us out of our daydreams. Within minutes, half the people on board were hanging over the railing vomiting. We would have joined them, but we hadn't had enough time for breakfast. At least the vomiting didn't last long. After about ten minutes of riding the waves, our boat turned east and entered an inside passage where the water was calmer. We were sailing through the Choushan Archipelago.

Putuoshan is one of over a hundred islands that make up the archipelago, and it's not the only one to which ships sail every day from Ningpo. Several of the larger islands were being developed for tourism. But Putoshan had been the destination of pilgrims for a thousand years. Of course, nowadays the island's visitors also include tourists in search of a place to relax and a place to breathe some fresh air for a change. But even tourists are aware of the merit they accrue from visiting such a place.

According to the *Surangama Sutra*, Kuan-yin was enlightened when she was able to see sound, when she broke through the limitations of the senses. Hence, her name Kuan-yin means "to see sound." As to whether she was an actual person or was invented to teach the interpenetration of our different means of perception, it's impossible to say. The important thing for Buddhist pilgrims is that Kuan-yin welcomes the faithful to Paradise, and it is not a bad idea to get acquainted beforehand, just in case one needs some extra help getting there. In addition to asking for Kuan-yin's help in the next life, pilgrims also came to Putuoshan to ask for a little compassion in this life, too.

As for the origin of Kuan-yin's association with the island, that went back to the ninth century and seems to be tied up with the island's location as the last point of land travelers see before they head out into the open sea, and also the first point of land they see when they return. During the eighth and ninth centuries, many Japanese monks came to China to study Buddhism, including Pure Land Buddhism, in which

Heart/Mind Rock

Kuan-yin figures prominently. Ningpo was the port they all used, and one day it happened that a Japanese monk carrying a statue of Kuan-yin back to Japan was shipwrecked on Putuoshan. He returned to Ningpo and tried again. But once more he was shipwrecked on the island. He tried again, and once more he ended up on the island. Hence, he came to the conclusion that Putuoshan must be Kuan-yin's home. In 863, he set up the first Kuan-yin shrine on the island and left his statue there. It wasn't long before the story of his repeated shipwrecks and Kuan-yin's connection with the island became known throughout China.

Our own arrival was much less eventful, other than the initial battle with the waves. Putuoshan was only a hundred kilometers from Ningpo, still it took five hours to get there. We were not alone in being glad to walk on dry land again. After disembarking, we went inside the harbor terminal and bought tickets for the night boat to Shanghai, and left our bags at the luggage depository. We had to be in Shanghai the next day and Hong Kong the following day and only had an afternoon to see the sights.

Rock That Flew Here

Just outside the boat terminal, we joined our fellow pilgrims and took a shuttle bus to Puchi Temple. Ten minutes later, we were there, on the other side of the island. Before going to see the temple, we decided we needed to recover from our boat trip and walked out to a nearby beach. It was called Hundred Step Beach. There were dozens of people wading in the water and playing in the sand. But it was the first day of November, and it was too cold to go swimming. We walked down to the south end of the beach and clambered onto some rocks, and worked our way around to a point of land that jutted into the sea. We found a comfortable spot and stretched out to enjoy the late fall sun. In front of us, we could see fishing boats sailing by on their way to cast their nets somewhere in the East China Sea. To our right, we could see the temple where the Japanese monk set up the first Kuan-yin shrine on the island a thousand years ago. Just below the temple was a cave, where the sea came crashing through and echoed Kuan-yin's name.

We could have sat there all day, but after sharing Steve's last joint we reluctantly walked back to Puchi Temple. This was where most people began their tour of the island. There were half a dozen major temples on Putuoshan and a dozen smaller ones, but Puchi was by far the biggest. Since our time on Putuoshan was limited to a single afternoon, we lit some incense and decided to walk the pilgrim trail that began just west of the temple. But first we bought pilgrim bags. The idea was to have one's bag chopped in the shrine hall of each temple along the trail as a testament of one's pilgrimage. After getting our bags chopped at Puchi, we set off. The person who sold us the bags said it took about ninety minutes to walk the whole trail, which was perfect. Our boat wasn't due to leave for three hours.

The trail was made of stone steps worn smooth by thousands upon thousands of pilgrims. About every ten minutes, we came to a different temple, and for one RMB we added another chop to our bags. In addition to the temples along the way, the trail also passed the island's two most famous rocks. The first was a sloping rock face onto which someone had carved the character *hsin* 心 for "mind" and painted it red. The character was so big several dozen people could sit on it at a time. The second rock was farther up the trail at the top of the ridge. It was another Rock That Flew Here, and it looked like it would fall over in a stiff breeze. But typhoons had come and gone, and it was still here, waiting to crush some unlucky pilgrim posing for a photo beneath it. The word *Omitofo* came to mind.

In the past, the island boasted more than two hundred temples and shrines. But during the 1950s, the island and its temples were requisitioned by the Chinese Navy for defense against a possible invasion by Taiwan. The Cultural Revolution of the '60s and '70s didn't help the island's temples either. But the 1980s finally saw a resumption of pilgrimage and the return of most of the island to the control of the Buddhists. Of course, the catch was that the monks and nuns who chose to live on the island were little more than caretakers. They were here to serve the hundreds and thousands of pilgrims and tourists, such as ourselves, who descended upon the island every day from Shanghai and Ningpo.

After covering our bags with chops, we eventually found ourselves back on the west side of the island. That was where the trail came down

View of East China Sea from Putuoshan

the mountain. It was just as well. It was a short walk from there to the harbor, where we enjoyed an early dinner and some very good seafood. The clams in basil were delicious. Afterwards, we reclaimed our bags and boarded our ship and said good-bye to Kuan-yin.

An hour later, our ship pulled out of the harbor, the sun went down, and we sat out on the deck. We sat there for hours and watched the stars light up the sky. We traced our journey south of the Yangtze from one star to the next. The line we traced went from Hong Kong's Kai Tak Airport to the stupa that contained Hui-neng's hair in Kuangchou, then across the Nanling Mountains to the trail of pilgrims and beggars on Hengshan, and the nonexistent paintings of Ch'i Pai-shih in Hsiangtan, and the homes of Mao Tse-tung and Liu Shao-ch'i, and the woman who choked on watermelon seeds at the Mawangtui Museum, and Tu Fu's weed-covered grave, and Ch'u Yuan's shrine on the Milo River, and the rocky promontory where the battle of Red Cliff was fought, and Wuhan's Yellow Crane Tower, and our night-long trip down the Yangtze, and the misty summit of Lushan, and the village where T'ao Yuan-ming discovered Peach Blossom Spring, and the mountain where Empty Cloud celebrated his 120th birthday, and the grave of Pa-ta Shan-jen, and China's porcelain capital of Chingtechen, and the inkstick and inkstone factories of Shehsien, and the scenic splendors of Huashan, and the Tiger Lady of Chiuhuashan, and Li Pai's grave, and the place where he embraced the moon, and the graves of Sun Yat-sen and the King of Borneo, and the Taoist mountain of Maoshan, and the teapot capital of Yihsing, and Hsu Hsia-k'o's grave, and the gardens of Suchou, and the hut where Stonehouse once lived, and Hangchou's West Lake, and Shaohsing's old wine, and Cold Mountain's cave, and Chiang Kai-shek's hometown, and the Buddha's skull, and the island home of Kuan-yin. We added it up. It looked like over 3,000 kilometers across the sky, across the sky and through the heart of China. What a trip. We couldn't wait to get home and tell our friends.

Lexicon

THE FOLLOWING LIST INCLUDES the modified Wade-Giles romanization used throughout this book for Chinese names, places, and terms. In each entry, the Wade-Giles romanization is followed by the Pinyin romanization and the traditional Chinese characters. Although the Wade-Giles system is no longer fashionable, it was designed as a compromise for speakers of various European languages in the mid- and late nineteenth century, while the Pinyin system was designed for Russian speakers in the mid-twentieth century.

Aichun / Aiqun / 愛群

Aikou/ Aikou / 隘口

Aiwanting / Aiwanting /
 愛晚亭

Amita / Amida / 阿彌陀

An Lu-shan / An Lushan /
 安祿山

Anhui / Anhui / 安徽

Anting / Anding / 安定

arhat / aluohan / 阿羅漢

Ayuwang / Ayuwang / 阿于王

Beijing / Beijing / 北京

Bodhidharma / Putidamo /
 普提達摩

Borneo / Boni / 渤泥

Brunei / Wencai / 文菜

Chaitoufeng / Chaitoufeng /
 釵頭鳳

Chang Chi / Zhang Ji / 張繼

Chang Chi-chih / Zhang Ji-zhi
 張即之

Chang Hsin-lan 張馨蘭

Chang Ta-ch'ien / Zhang
 Daqian / 張大千

Changchiang / Changjiang / 長江

Changnan / Changnan / 昌南

Changsha / Changsha / 長沙

Changshu / Changshu / 常熟

Ch'ang-an / Chang'an / 長安

Ch'ang-ta / Changda / 常達

Chantanlin / Zhantanlin / 旃檀林

Chekiang / Zhejiang / 浙江

Chenchueh / Zhenjue / 真覺

Chenju / Zhenru / 真如

Cheng (river) / Zheng / 蒸

Cheng Ho / Zheng He / 鄭和

Ch'i (state) / Qi / 齊

Ch'i Pai-shih / Qi Baishi / 齊白石

Chi-kung / Jigong / 濟公

Ch'i-fo / Qifo / 奇佛

ch'i-kung / qigong / 氣功

Chiang Ching-kuo / Jiang Jingguo / 蔣經國

Chiang Hsiao-wu / Jiang Xiaowu / 蔣孝武

Chiang Kai-shek / Jiang Jieshi / 蔣介石

Chiangnan / Jiangnan / 江南

Chiehtou / Jietou / 街頭

Ch'ien Shao-wu / Qian Shaowu / 錢紹武

Chienhu / Jianhu / 鑒湖

Chientang / Qiantang / 錢塘

Chih-yi / Zhiyi / 智顗

chih-yin / zhiyin / 知音

Chihpi / Chibi / 赤壁

Chihyuan / Zhiyuan / 祇園

Chin Ch'iao-chueh / Jin Qiaojue / 金喬覺

Ch'in (dynasty) / Qin / 秦

Ch'ing (dynasty) / Qing / 清

Ch'ing-kung / Qinggong / 清珙

Chingchuan / Qingchuan / 晴川

Chinghsien / Jingxian / 涇縣

Chingshan / Chingshan / 青山

Chingte / Jingde / 景德

Chingtechen / Jingdezhen / 景德鎮

Chingtzu / Jingzi / 淨慈

Chingyunpu / Qingyunpu / 青雲圃

Chinhuai / Jinhuai / 秦淮

Chiuchiang / Jiujiang / 九江

Chiuchin / Jiujin / 虬津

Chiuhsiao Wanfukung / Jiuxiao
   Wanfugong / 九霄萬福宮

Chiuhuashan / Jiuhuashan /
   九花山

Chiulungchuan / Jiulongquan /
   九龍泉

Chiutzushan / Jiuzishan /
   九子山

Ch'iu Chin / Qiu Jin / 秋瑾

Chou (dynasty) / Zhou / 周

Chou En-lai / Zhou Enlai /
   周恩來

Choushan / Zhoushan / 舟山

Chu Ch'uan / Zhu Quan / 朱權

Chu Hsi / Zhu Xi / 朱熹

Chu Ta / Zhu Da / 朱耷

Chu Ying-t'ai / Zhu Yingtai /
   祝英台

Ch'u (state) / Chu / 楚

Ch'u Yuan / Qu Yuan / 屈原

Chu-jung Huo-shen /
   Zhurong Huoshen / 祝融火神

Chu-ko Liang / Zhuge Liang /
   諸葛亮

Chuang Yen / Zhuang Yan /
   莊嚴

Chuang-tzu / Zhuangzi / 莊子

Chuchiang / Qujiang / 曲江

Chung Tzu-ch'i / Zhong Ziqi /
   鐘子期

Chung Yung / Zhong Yong /
   仲雍

Chung-shan / Zhongshan / 中山

Chungnan / Zhongnan / 終南

Chunghuamen /
   Zhonghuamen / 中華門

Chuhuatai / Juhuatai / 菊花台

Chunshan / Junshan / 君山

Chushan / Zhushan / 珠山

Chutang / Chutang / 楚塘

Chutzuchou / Juzizhou /
   橘子洲

Dogen / Daoyuan / 道元

Fang (layman) / Fang / 方

Feilaishih / Feilaishi / 飛來石

Feng-kan / Fenggan / 豐干

Fenghua / Fenghua / 奉化

Fu-hsing / Fuxing / 馥馨

Fushan / Fushan / 府山

Fuyen / Fuyan / 福嚴

Han (river, dynasty) / Han / 漢

Han-shan (poet) / Hanshan /
   寒山

Hankou / Hankou / 漢口

Huanyou Laojen / Huanyou
  Laoren / 幻遊老人

Huashan / Huashan / 華山

Huayen / Huayan / 華嚴

Huchou / Huzhou / 湖州

Hui-neng / Huineng / 慧能

Hui-shen / Huishen / 慧深

Hui-ssu / Huisi / 慧思

Hui-yuan / Huiyuan / 慧遠

Huichou / Huizhou / 徽州

Huiyenfeng / Huiyanfeng /
  回雁峰

Hukou / Hukou / 湖口

Hunan / Hunan /湖南

Hung Hsiu-ch'uan /
  Hong Xiuquan / 洪秀全

Hung-jen / Hongren / 弘忍

Hung-wu / Hongwu / 洪武

Hunghu / Honghu / 洪湖

Hupei / Hubei / 湖北

Hupin / Hubin / 湖濱

Hutien / Hutian / 湖田

Jenmin / Renmin / 人民

Joushen Paodien /
  Roushen Baodian / 肉身寶殿

Kai Tak / Qide / 啟德

Kaifeng / Kaifeng / 開封

Kan (river) / Gan / 贛

Kao Chih-hsi / Gao Zhixi /
  高至喜

Kao Yung-k'uei / Gao Yongkui /
  高永奎

Kaoling / Gaoling / 高嶺

Kiangsi / Jiangsi / 江西

Kiangsu / Jiangsu / 江蘇

k'o / ke / 柯

Koshan / Keshan / 科山

Kou Chien / Gou Jian / 勾踐

Koupuli / Goubuli / 狗不理

Ku Ching-chou / Gu Jingzhou /
  顧景舟

Kuaichishan / Kuaijishan /
  會稽山

Kuan-kung / Guangong / 關公

Kuan-yin / Guanyin / 觀音

Kuanchien / Guanqian / 觀前

Kuangchou / Guangzhou / 廣州

Kuanghsiao / Guangxiao / 光孝

Kuangsi / Guangxi / 廣西

Kuangtung / Guangdong / 廣東

Kuantang / Guantang / 官塘

Kueilin / Guilin / 桂林

Kueiyuankuan / Guiyuanguan /
  奎元館

Kunlun / Kunlun / 崑崙

kuo-pa / guoba / 鍋巴

Kuoching / Guoqing / 國清

Kuo-yi / Guoyi / 果一

Kushan / Gushan / 孤山

Lanting / Lanting / 蘭亭

lao-chiu / lao-jiu / 老酒

Lao-tzu / Laozi / 老子

Lei Tsu / Lei Zu / 縲祖

Leifeng / Leifeng / 雷峰

Leitienchen / Leitianzhen / 雷甸鎮

Li Ch'ang-hung / Li Changhong / 李昌鴻

Li Mi / Li Mi / 李密

Li Pai / Li Bai / 李白

Li T'ing-kuei / Li Tinggui / 李廷珪

Liang Shan-po / Liang Shanbo / 梁山伯

Liangchu / Liangzhu / 梁祝

Lienhuafeng / Lianhuafeng / 蓮花峰

Lin Ho-ching / Lin Hejing / 林和靖

Lin Piao / Lin Biao / 林彪

Linchuan / Linchuan / 臨川

Lingnan / Lingnan / 嶺南

Lingyin / Lingyin / 零隱

Liu Cheng-ch'uan / Liu Zhengquan / 劉正泉

Liu Shao-ch'i / Liu Shaoqi / 劉少奇

Liuhua / Liuhua / 流花

Liujung / Liurong / 六榕

Liuyuan / Liuyuan / 留園

Louwailou / Louyailou / 樓外樓

Loyang / Luoyang / 洛陽

Lu Hsun / Lu Xun / 魯迅

Lu You / Lu You / 陸游

Lulin / Lulin 盧林

Lungching / Longjing / 籠井

Lungshan / Longshan / 龍山

Lungweishan / Longweishan / 龍尾山

Lushan / Lushan 盧山

Ma-anshan / Ma'anshan / 馬鞍山

Ma-ku / Magu / 麻姑

Ma-tsu / Mazu / 馬祖

Machen / Mazhen / 馬鎮

Maitreya / Mile / 彌樂

Manchu / Manzu / 滿族

Manjusri / Manjusri / 文殊

Mao Meng / Mao Meng / 茅蒙

Mao Tse-tung / Mao Zedong / 毛澤東

Maochien / Maojian / 毛劍

Maoshan / Maoshan / 茅山

Mawangtui / Mawangdui / 馬王堆

Milo / Miluo / 汨羅

Ming (dynasty) / Ming / 明

Mingyen / Mingyan / 明巖

Mokanshan / Moganshan / 莫干山

Nanchang / Nanchang / 南昌

Nanlin / Nanlin / 南林

Nanling / Nanling / 南嶺

Nantai / Nantai / 南台

Nantienmen / Nantianmen / 南天門

Nanyueh / Nanyue / 南岳

Nengjen / Nengren / 能忍

Ning (prince) / Ning / 寧

Ninghsiang / Ningxiang / 寧鄉

Ningpo / Ningbo / 寧波

Nora Sun / Sun Suifen / 孫穗芬

Omeishan / Emeishan / 鵝眉山

Omitofo / Amituofo / 阿彌陀佛

Pa-ta Shan-jen / Bada Shanren / 八大山人

Pai Chu-yi / Bai Juyi / 白局易

Pailutung Shuyuan / Bailutong Shuyuan / 白鹿洞書院

Paiti / Baiti / 白堤

Paiyunlou / Paiyunlou / 排雲樓

Paiyunshan / Baiyunshan / 白雲山

Pao Y.K. / Bao Yugang / 包玉剛

Pao-t'an / Baotan / 寶曇

P'eng (bird) / Peng / 鵬

P'eng Te-huai / Peng Dehuai / 彭德懷

Pingchiang / Pingjiang / 平江

Pingchiao / Pingqiao / 平橋

Poyanghu / Boyanghu / 鄱陽湖

P'u-hsien / Puxian / 普賢

Puchi (town) / Puqi / 蒲圻

Puchi (temple) / Puji / 普濟

Pukou / Pukou / 蒲口

Putuoshan / Putuoshan / 普陀山

sanpan / sanban / 三板

Sanweiyuan / Sanweiyuan / 三味院

Shan (river) / Shan / 剡

Shangfeng / Shangfeng / 上封

shao (music) / shao / 韶

Shaofeng / Shaofeng / 韶峰

Shaohsing / Shaoxing / 紹興.

Shaolin / Shaolin / 少林

Shaoshan / Shaoshan / 韶山

Shehsien / Shexian / 歙縣

Shen (garden) / Shen / 沈

Shenchen / Shenzhen / 深圳

Shennungchia / Shennongjia / 神農架

Shih-te / Shide / 拾得

Shih-t'ou / Shitou / 石頭

Shih-wu / Shiwu / 石屋

Shihfeng / Shifeng / 始奉

Shihhsinfeng / Shixinfeng /
　始信峰

Shihku / Shigu / 石鼓

Shou-yeh / Shouye / 壽冶

Shu-liao / Shuliao / 樗寮

Shun (emperor) / Shun / 舜

Shushan / Shushan / 屬山

Sian / Xi'an / 西安

Ssukuchuanshu /
　Sikuquanshu / 四庫全書

Su Tung-p'o / Su Dongpo /
　蘇東坡

Subhuti / Xuputi / 須菩提

Suchou / Suzhou / 蘇州

Sui (dynasty) / Sui 隋

Suichou / Suizhou / 隨州

Sun Ch'o / Sun Chuo / 孫綽

Sun Yat-sen / Sun Yixian /
　孫逸仙

Sung (dynasty) / Song / 宋

Sung Mei-ling / Song Meiling /
　宋美齡

Sungholou / Songhelou /
　松鶴樓

Sungshan / Songshan / 嵩山

Surangama / Lengyan / 楞嚴

Tachien (alley) / Daqian / 大監

Tachuchiu / Daqujiu / 大曲酒

Taichichuan / Taijiquan /
　太極拳

Taihu / Taihu / 人湖

Taiping (reservoir, rebels) /
　Taiping / 太平

Taiping Tienkuo / Taiping
　Tianguo / 太平天國

Taishan / Taishan / 泰山

Tangtu / Dangtu / 當涂

Tatung / Datong / 大同

T'ang (dynasty) / Tang / 唐

T'ang Ch'ing-hai / Tang
　Qinghai / 湯清海

T'ang Hsien-tsu /
　Tang Xianzu / 湯顯祖

T'ang Wan / Tang Wan / 唐婉

Tangkou / Tangkou / 湯口

T'ao Hung-ching /
　T'ao Hongjing / 陶弘景

T'ao Yuan-ming /
　Tao Yuanming / 陶原明

Tao-jung / Daorong / 道容

Tao-yi / Daoyi / 道一

Taochangshan /
　Daochangshan / 道場山

Taoteching / Daodejing / 道德經

Te-an / De'an / 德安

Teching / Deqing / 德清

Teng Hsiao-p'ing / Deng
Xiaoping / 鄧小平

Tengwangke / Tengwangge /
滕王閣

Ti-tsang / Dizang / 地藏

Tienchin / Tianjin / 天津

Tienningkuan / Tianningguan /
天寧觀

Tientai / Tiantai / 天台

Tientaishan / Tiantaishan /
天台山

Tientung / Tiantong / 天童

Tienwangchen /
Tianwangzhen / 天王鎮

Tienyiko / Tianyige / 天一閣

Tinglienfang / Dinglianfang /
丁蓮芳

Tingshan / Dingshan / 丁山

Tingshu / Dingshu / 丁屬

Tsai Eh / Cai E / 蔡鍔

Tsaikenhsiang / Caigenxiang /
菜根香

Tsaishih / Caishi / 采石

Ts'ao Ts'ao / Cao Cao / 曹操

Tseng Hou-yi / Zeng Houyi /
曾侯乙

Tu Fu / Du Fu / 杜甫

Tuanwuchieh / Duanwujie /
段午節

Tung Ch'i-ch'ang /
Dong Qichang / 董其昌

Tunglin / Donglin / 東林

Tungtejen / Tongderen / 同德仁

Tungting / Dongting / 洞庭

Tunhsi / Tunxi / 屯溪

Tzuchinshan / Zijinshan /
紫金山

tz'u-ch'i / ciqi / 磁器

wai-kuo-jen / waiguoren /
外國人

Wang Hsi-chih / Wang Xizhi /
王羲之

Wang Yang-ming / Wang
Yangming / 王陽明

Wangshih / Wangshi / 网師

Wangssu / Wangsi / 王四

Wanshou / Wanshou / 萬壽

Wen-shu / Wenshu / 文殊

Wu (state) / Wu / 吳

Wu-en / Wu'en / 晤恩

Wuchang / Wuchang / 武昌

Wuchou / Wuzhou / 梧州

Wuhan / Wuhan / 武漢

Wuhsi / Wuxi / 無錫

Wukang / Wukang / 武康

Wuling / Wuling / 武嶺